BLESSINGS OF KHILĀFAT

(An English rendering of Barakāt-e-Khilāfat)

BLESSINGS OF KHILĀFAT

(An English rendering of Barakāt-e-Khilāfat)

by

Ḥaḍrat Khalīfatul-Masīḥ II,
Mirza Bashirud-Din Mahmud Ahmad
(may Allah be pleased with him)

Addresses Delivered During the Annual Convention of 1914

Blessings of Khilāfat

An English rendering of:
Barakāt-e-Khilāfat

Translated from Urdu into English by:
Ahmad Mustansir Qamar

First English translation published in UK: 2013

Published by:
Islam International Publications Ltd.
Islamabad, Sheephatch Lane
Tilford, Surrey GU10 2AQ
United Kingdom

Printed in UK at:
Raqeem Press
Islamabad, Tilford, Surrey

For further information you may visit www.alislam.org.

ISBN: 978-1-84880-088-5

ABOUT THE AUTHOR

Ḥaḍrat Muṣleḥ-e-Mau'ūd, Mirza Bashirud-Din Mahmud Ahmad[ra] was the Promised Son and the second *Khalīfah* of the Promised Messiah[as], the Holy Founder of the Ahmadiyya Muslim Community. Born in accordance with a mighty prophecy of the Promised Messiah[as], he was gifted with knowledge, both secular and divine. His understanding of the Holy Quran and Islamic matters was immense. He wrote a detailed commentary covering several chapters of the Holy Quran. His books and lectures are replete with points of wisdom and understanding. He was the prince of exposition—both in writing and speech. He was filled with the light Divine.

In 1914, at the age of 25, he was elected as *Khalīfah*, that is, successor, to the Promised Messiah[as]. For 52 years he led the Community and served the causes for which it was established. He inspired and motivated his followers' spiritual development; he spoke and wrote in defence of Islam; and he established institutions to propagate Islam all over the world.

CONTENTS

About The Author .... *v*

Publisher's Note .... *ix*

Introduction .... *xiii*

First Speech: Blessings of Khilāfat **1**

Importance of Using Appropriate Terminology and Etiquettes ... 3

Heavy Burden of Khilāfat 5

Functions of Khilāfat 9

Misunderstandings About Khilāfat 10

Resemblance with Earlier Khilāfats 13

Pertinent Incidents 20

Dire Consequences of Abandoning the Robe of Khilāfat 27

Has Khilāfat Assumed a Hereditary Characteristic? 29

Path of Reconciliation 33

Further Heavenly Testimonies About Impending Issues of Khilāfat 47

Important Issues Facing the Jamā'at 68

Politics 70

Marriage between Aḥmadīs and non-Aḥmadīs and Issue of Kufw 92

Prayer in Congregation 114

Zakat 117
The Life History of the Promised Messiah[as] 122
Other Important Issues 124

Second Speech: Objects of Human Life 133

Importance of the Subject 134
Attaining Nearness to Allah 138
Beauty and Grandeur of Allah and His Kingdom 144
No Associate with God 156
Perform Good Deeds with Noble Intentions 158
Objective of Islam 165
Stages of Spiritual Development 166
Seven Ranks of Spiritual Development 167
A Misunderstanding 181

Glossary *187*
Index *193*

PUBLISHER'S NOTE

According to our system of counting Quranic verses, the verse *Bismillāhhir-Raḥmānir-Raḥīm* (In the name of Allah, the Most Gracious, Ever Merciful) is counted as the first verse of the chapter, which it precedes. Some publishers of the Holy Quran however, begin counting following *Bismillāhhir-Raḥmānir-Raḥīm*. Should the reader not find the relevant verse under the number mentioned in this book, he or she is advised to deduct 1 from the number. For example, if this book quotes Ch. 35: *al-Fāṭir:* 25, then some copies of the Holy Quran will list the same verse under Ch. 35: *al-Fāṭir:* 24.

Where necessary, translation of the Arabic text has been elaborated by additional words to explain the meaning. Such words are not in italics. The word *and* at the commencement of a translated verse has been omitted.

The form *ibn* has been used in both initial and medial position in the names of persons, in order to conform to current usage, although *bin* also occurs medially in some original texts (abbreviated usually as *b.*).

Quotations from the Holy Bible are from the King James Translation.

The name of Muhammad[sa], the Holy Prophet of Islam, has been followed by the symbol [sa], which is an abbreviation for the prayer (صلی اللہ علیہ وسلم) *ṣallallāhu 'alaihi wasallam* (may peace and blessings of Allah be upon him). The names of other Prophets[as] and messengers are followed by the symbol [as], an abbreviation for (علیہ السلام/ علیہم السلام) *'alaihissalām/'alaihimussalām* (on whom be peace). The actual prayers have not generally been set out in full, but they should nevertheless, be understood as being repeated in full in each case. The symbol [ra] is used with the name of the Companions of the Holy Prophet[sa] and those of the Promised Messiah[as]. It stands for (رضی اللہ عنہ / رضی اللہ عنہا / رضی اللہ عنہم) *raḍī allāhu 'anhu/'anhā/'anhum* (may Allah be pleased with him/with her/with them). [rh] stands for (رحمہ اللہ تعالیٰ) *raḥimahullāhu ta'ālā* (may Allah's blessing be on him). [aa] stands for (ایدہ اللہ تعالیٰ) *ayyadahullāhu ta'ālā binaṣrihil-azīz* (may Allah, the Almighty help him).

In transliterating Arabic words we have followed the following system adopted by the Royal Asiatic Society:

ا at the beginning of a word, pronounced as *a*, *i*, *u* preceded by a very slight aspiration, like *h* in the English word *honour*.

ث *th*, pronounced like *th* in the English word *thing*.

ح *ḥ*, a guttural aspirate, stronger than *h*.

خ *kh*, pronounced like the Scotch *ch* in *loch*.

ذ *dh*, pronounced like the English *th* in *that*.

ص *ṣ*, strongly articulated *s*.

ض *ḍ*, similar to the English *th* in *this*.

ط *ṭ*, strongly articulated palatal *t*.

ظ *ẓ*, strongly articulated *z*.

ع ', a strong guttural, the pronunciation of which must be learnt by the ear.

غ *gh*, a sound approached very nearly in the *r grasseye* in French, and in the German *r*. It requires the muscles of the throat to be in the 'gargling' position whilst pronouncing it.

ق *q*, a deep guttural *k* sound.

ئ ', a sort of catch in the voice.

Short vowels are represented by:

a for ـــَـــ (like *u* in *bud*)
i for ـــِـــ (like *i* in *bid*)
u for ـــُـــ (like *oo* in *wood*)

Long vowels by:

ā for ـــاـــ or آ (like *a* in *father*);
ī for ى ـــِـــ or ـــٖـــ (like *ee* in *deep*);
ū for و ـــُـــ (like *oo* in *root*);

Other:

ai for ى ـــَـــ (like *i* in *site*)[1];
au for و ـــَـــ (resembling *ou* in *sound*)

Please note that in transliterated words the letter *e* is to be pronounced as in *prey* which rhymes with *day*; however the pronunciation is flat without the element of English diphthong. If in Urdu and Persian words *e* is lengthened a bit more, it is

---

1 In Arabic words like شيخ (Shaikh) there is an element of diphthong which is missing when the word is pronounced in Urdu.

transliterated as *ei* to be pronounced as *ei* in *feign* without the element of diphthong. Thus کے is transliterated as *kei*. For the nasal sound of *n* we have used the symbol *ń*. Thus the Urdu word میں is transliterated as *meiń*.[2]

The consonants not included in the above list have the same phonetic value as in the principal languages of Europe.

We have not transliterated Arabic words which have become part of English language, e.g., Islam, Mahdi, Quran[3], Hijra, Ramadan, hadith, ulema, umma, sunna, kafir, pukka, etc.

Curved commas are used in the system of transliteration, ‘ for ع, ’ for ء. Commas as punctuation marks are used according to the normal usage. Similarly, normal usage is followed for the apostrophe.

---

[2] These transliterations are not included in the system of transliteration by The Royal Asiatic Society.

[3] Concise Oxford Dictionary records Quran in three forms—Quran, Quran and Koran.

INTRODUCTION

We are honoured to publish the first English rendering of the speeches delivered by Ḥaḍrat Khalīfatul-Masīḥ II Mirza Bashirud-Din Mahmud Ahmad[ra] at *Jalsah Sālānah* [Annual Convention], Qadian, in December, 1914, soon after he had been appointed by Allah the Almighty to the august office of *Khalīfatul-Masīḥ*.

It was a time when the Jamā'at [Community] faced serious challenges. After the demise of Ḥaḍrat Maulānā Nurud-Din[ra], the first *Khalīfah* of the Promised Messiah[as], efforts to undermine the institution of *Khilāfat* gained momentum under the leadership of Maulavī Muhammad Ali and Khawaja Kamalud-Din, once counted among distinguished companions of the Promised Messiah[as]. Opponents of the institution of *Khilāfat* favoured shifting the administrative powers of the *Khalīfah* to the Anjuman, a body of executives that had been established by the Promised Messiah[as] to implement and supervise the day-to-day affairs of the Jamā'at. Allah the Almighty, in accordance with His glad tidings which the Promised Messiah[as] had recorded in *al-Waṣiyyat*, protected the Community and established it firmly, once again, on the institution of *Khilāfat* under the leadership of Ḥaḍrat Mirza Bashirud-Din Mahmud Ahmad[ra].

It was in this historical backdrop that Ḥaḍrat Mirza Bashirud-Din Mahmud Ahmad[ra] made these speeches. These speeches were delivered during the proceedings of *Jalsah Sālānah* Qadian in 1914, since this was a time when the faithful arrived in Qadian in large numbers from all over the sub-continent to see their beloved Imam and listen to his instructions. Having elaborated on the subject of *Khilāfat* with references to the Holy Quran and Bible and successfully making his point that *Khilāfat* was a divine institution and the *Khalīfah* a manifestation of the power of God, he touched on a number of other important issues the Jamā'at was facing at that time.

The first speech was largely devoted to the refutation of the allegation of *anti-Khilāfat* elements and elucidation of the spiritual station a *Khalīfah* of the Prophet of time possesses. The second part of the speech delivered in the afternoon highlighted the importance of congregational prayer, and preservation of the life history of the Promised Messiah[as] on authentic lines. He also spoke in detail on his views regarding the issues such as interfaith marriages and the question of parity between the marital partners. Also, he laid down precious guidelines for the Jamā'at in relation to their involvement in politics. In his speech on the second day of the *Jalsah*, he expounded his commentary on the *Āyatul-Kursī* and spoke on the seven stages of man's spiritual development that, if completed, eventually make him the beloved of his Lord.

The book was translated from Urdu into English by Ahmad Mustansir Qamar and was first revised by Mirza Anas Ahmad. The translation was prepared for publication under the guidance of Additional Wakālat-e-Taṣnīf by its English Translation section, based in the U.S.A. Thanks are due to Munawar Ahmed Saeed,

Luqman Tahir Mahmood, Kashif Hussain Baloch, Amina Maryem Shams and others. It may be noted that the speeches, as delivered, were not divided into sections. The headings given in this translation are from the translators.

May God Almighty enable us all to derive the utmost benefit from these speeches and help us become truly practicing Aḥmadīs. *Āmīn*.

Munir-ud-Din Shams
Additional Wakīlut-Taṣnīf
London, July 2013

FIRST SPEECH:

BLESSINGS OF KHILĀFAT

(December 27, 1914)

بِسۡمِ اللّٰهِ الرَّحۡمٰنِ الرَّحِيۡمِ
نَحۡمَدُهٗ وَ نُصَلِّیۡ عَلٰی رَسُوۡلِهِ الۡكَرِيۡمِ [1]

After reciting *tashahhud, ta'awwudh,* and *Sūrah al-Fātiḥah,* Ḥuḍūr[ra] said:

I would like to speak to you about a few important points, one of which, in my opinion, is the only means of establishing not only Aḥmadiyyat but also Islam; and without which no human being can ever establish a relationship with God, nor can a person become a true Muslim. Moreover, no one can acquire it unless he is a recipient of God's special grace and blessing.

Besides this, there are a few other important matters, but they are not as vital. With Allah's grace and blessings, I will, God willing, expound tomorrow on a topic which is of vital importance and about which I have been anxious to communicate for a long time.

---

[1] In the name of Allah, the Gracious, the Merciful; we praise Him and invoke blessings upon His Noble Messenger.

Today I would like to speak on a few initial points, which, though not as important, are nevertheless essential to be conveyed. The reason why I am leaving the more important topic for tomorrow is that when a blessing is granted without any effort on the part of the recipient, it is usually taken for granted. By deferring the important point until tomorrow, I wish to achieve another objective, namely that only those should have the opportunity to listen to it who will stay here till tomorrow sincerely wishing to listen to it, because a blessing which is received without any striving is not appreciated as much as the one for which one strives.

I am suffering from a cough and my voice has grown weak. I request that everyone should keep sitting patiently. Even if my voice does not reach all of you, the reward will definitely be given to all who are present here.

People hear many things, but may not necessarily be influenced by what they hear. Yet they share the blessings of the place where they are sitting. What it comes down to is that it is not necessary that a listener of good words should always be guided. But it has also been observed that a person can receive guidance merely by visiting a holy place without really being involved in any discussion. Therefore, even if my voice fails to reach everyone, Allah will surely bless you with guidance in view of your sincerity and steadfastness, if you remain seated.

Now, before I come to the point at issue, I would like to address a few issues which are being raised often and to speak on which has become increasingly important.

Importance of Using Appropriate Terminology and Etiquettes

Just yesterday, on my way here, I came across some people who appeared to be peasant farmers. They greeted me by saying: '*O, Prophet of God! Peace be on you.*' From their way of greeting me, it is obvious that they simply do not know what a Prophet really is. I am not in the habit of directly pointing out the mistakes made by people; rather, I feel very uncomfortable if I ever have to do so. Firstly, because the person may feel embarrassed. Secondly, I myself feel greatly embarrassed to reprove someone for his mistakes. Therefore, I usually mention the errors committed by people in general terms and do not point to a particular person except in the case of those with whom I enjoy a special relationship. With them, I talk in private.

You must remember that a Prophet is someone who has been granted the title of a Prophet and no one else. There is no doubt, however, that God has granted us the opportunity to serve a Prophet. Therefore, revere the Prophets of God as they must be revered and do not count others as equal to them. The Holy Quran records the names of many of God's Prophets. Moreover, you also know the name of the Prophet sent by God in this age. Therefore, other than these, the rest of the people are only brothers to each other. However, for the progress of the Jamā'at, God has established the institution of *Khilāfat*. The person who has been assigned that responsibility is none other than a brother of yours; to call him a Prophet is not at all permissible.

Some people extend their hands to touch my knees and feet. They do so with fervour of love and devotion and not with the intent of idolatry; yet, such practices can lead to idolatry. A reference has been made to this effect in the *Bukhārī* where Ibne Abbas[ra] relates that the idols of the people of Noah that are mentioned in the Holy Quran are in fact the names of the elders of the infidels. Their successors desired that memorials be set up in the memory for their elders, so that people remember them and follow their examples. For this purpose, they erected their statues. But when the later generations observed their forefathers paying respects to these statues, they started to revere them even more than their forefathers. In time, the statues garnered even more reverence. Consequently, a time came when people started prostrating before the statues, forgetting the real station of those elders, and instead making them partners with God. In short, some immoral acts seem minor and harmless in the beginning, but can lead to lasting and irreversible damage.

My own nature and disposition is such that I do not like that people should kiss my hands. People used to kiss the hands of the Promised Messiah[as] and he did not forbid them. From this, I understood that this could be allowed. But, I failed to reason this out. Then I saw people kissing the hands of Khalīfatul-Masīḥ I[ra] about whom the Promised Messiah[as] has said, 'He walks in step with me'. He was my tutor as well as Khalīfatul-Masīḥ. To me, his action constituted a decisive verdict in itself. But I got full satisfaction, and an undeniable argument, when I learned that the companions of the Holy Prophet[sa] used to kiss his hands and take them to their eyes. Now, although I do not stop those who kiss my hands, I do get embarrassed when I see them doing so. And the only reason why I do not forbid them from doing this is that they do it merely out of their fervour of love and fidelity. In any case, these things should not exceed due limits, for then they may take the semblance of idolatry.

Heavy Burden of Khilāfat

Now, I wish to speak on another subject, which is *Khilāfat.* One may say that a lot has already been heard in this regard and that the same has been repeated here for a couple of days. Hence, people feel compelled to ask when this debate will finally come to an end.

As a matter of fact, what you have already heard about *Khilāfat* has been stated by those whose position is no different than a passerby witnessing an incident. Listen! the description of an illness that a patient gives himself is bound to be very different from the description given by a person who merely looks after the patient as an attendant. Similarly, some people have related to you things according to their own knowledge and understanding. But what I am going to narrate to you is based on my personal experience and not what I have heard from people. However one may describe the condition of another person's pain and suffering, it can never be as accurate as that which is described by the patient himself. Therefore, whatever I have undergone can best be described by me alone.

To an onlooker, it might seem great to rule over a community of millions. But, you must reflect—for God's sake—whether, after my gaining authority, your freedom has suffered in the least as compared to the past? Do I treat you like slaves or rule over you like a king or look down upon you as if you are my subordinates or prisoners? Generally speaking, is there any difference between you and those who have turned away from *Khilāfat*? There seems to be no difference. Yet, you should remember that there is one big difference! And that is that:

> **You have someone who has true sympathy for you; who truly loves you; who considers your pain and sufferings to be his own; and who is always praying to Allah for you.**

The group opposed to us have no one to do this on their behalf. You have someone who is always anxious for your well-being, who puts himself into trouble for your sake, and who prays restlessly before his Lord for the sake of your comfort and peace. But they have none who can ever do this on their behalf. Having to take care of only one person renders one restless. Can you imagine the condition of a person who has to look after not only hundreds but millions of people who suffer from diverse problems? Therefore, you should know that your freedom has not been impinged upon in any way. On the contrary, a heavy burden of responsibilities has been placed, for your sake, upon someone who was as free as you.

I hear that some people say that I wanted to rule, and that by creating a division within the Jamā'at I have made people get initiated at my hand. I must tell you how I felt at the time of the initiation. I felt myself staggering and under a huge burden when the ceremony ended. At that moment, I pondered over it and reflected deeply if there was some way of retreating from this position, but couldn't find one. After that, for many days, I continuously tried to think of some way to retract. It was then that God showed me in a vision that I was walking up a hill and became greatly worried because of the difficulties involved along the way and decided to return. When I turned around to move backwards, I found the mountain to be standing like a wall in my way blocking all possibilities of return. I understood thereby that God had conveyed to me that I could only move forwards, and that I could not withdraw from my position.

I have given much thought to the point as to why Prophethood is bestowed upon a Prophet after he is at least forty years of age. I have realized that man lives only for a short time after he is forty. This realization gives strength to a Prophet to face the impending difficulties. But were this responsibility to be bestowed upon him when he was young, it would prove to be very difficult for him. Spending so many years of such a difficult life would become extremely hard for him as this is never an easy task.

An ember appears beautiful from a distance but the reality of it is known only to the person holding it in his hand. Similarly, *Khilāfat* appears to be something very delightful, and the ignorant beholders think that the *Khalīfah* has achieved something wonderful. But they do not know that the thing which looks beautiful to them is in fact a huge burden, and that without being a recipient of God's special grace one is simply unable to carry this burden.

The word *Khalīfah* is used for the one who continues the work of his predecessor. About the person whose work the *Khalīfah* carries forward, God Almighty says in the Holy Quran:[2]

---

2 *Sūrah al-Inshirāḥ*, 94:3–4

وَوَضَعْنَا عَنْكَ وِزْرَكَ ۝ الَّذِيْٓ اَنْقَضَ ظَهْرَكَ ۝

That is: We have removed from you your burden which had *well nigh* broken your back. When God Himself has clearly stated that the Holy Prophet's back was about to be broken by this burden, then who else can stay strong after having been burdened with such a task? However, the same God, who lightened the burden of the Holy Prophet[sa] and who also enabled a person to carry such burden successfully in this age, strengthens the backs of those who propagate His faith after the time of the Prophet. I was always suffering from one ailment or another even before I became *Khalīfah*, but now you have seen that since the day of my election, I have felt well only on a few days. If I was really so jubilant to have attained *Khilāfat* and had desired it, I should have become healthier and put on much weight after attaining it. Had I been trying to acquire it for the last six years, as those who do not believe in *Khilāfat* allege, I should have become healthier by now with the joy of having achieved it. But that is not the case. In my childhood, whenever my mother expressed anxiety on account of my ill health, the Promised Messiah[as] would say "He will become healthier when he experiences some happiness", and would quote the example of Khawaja [Kamalud-Din] that he too was very lean before passing the law examination. Having come to know that he had passed the examination, he put on a lot of weight in the course of a very short time. So if *Khilāfat* has been an empire that I am really so happy to attain, then I should have become healthier upon acquiring it. But those who keep company with me and are familiar with my life know very well of the difficult times I pass through. The pain that I suffer is known only to me.

Functions of Khilāfat

The issue of *Khilāfat* is not a complex one. In my speech on 12th April, 1914.[3] I had explained with reference to a verse from the Holy Quran what the function of a *Khalīfah* is. The word *Khalīfah* means someone who succeeds another and continues the work of his predecessor. To understand the function of a successor, one has to look at the function of the predecessor. God has explained the work of the Holy Prophet, peace and blessings of Allah be upon him, as following:[4]

... يَتْلُوْا عَلَيْهِمْ اٰيٰتِهٖ وَ يُزَكِّيْهِمْ وَ يُعَلِّمُهُمُ الْكِتٰبَ وَالْحِكْمَةَ ...

That is, he should

1. Recite the verses of God to the people,
2. Purify them,
3. Teach them the book and
4. Impart wisdom to them.

I also explained that these four tasks of the Prophet cannot be performed by any 'Anjuman'. They can be performed only by the person whom God Himself appoints after the Prophet, and who is entitled as *Khalīfah*. I do not wish to go into details about this subject right now. For the time being, I will take up a few key

[3] The speech has been published under the title: *Manṣab-e-Khilāfat*.

[4] *Sūrah Āl-e-'Imrān*, 3:165

accusations against me and answer them. I will also explain why I did not give up my courage and determination, and remained steadfast in my stance.

Some people criticize me by saying that I should have shown a big heart and declined the office of *Khilāfat*. Someone who talks like this considers *Khilāfat* to be a source of great pleasure and happiness; what he does not know is that *Khilāfat* has no worldly comforts and pleasures.

I will now explain why, having gathered all my courage and bravery, I took up this task. What exactly it was which, upon seeing the community divided into two, gave me the heart to stay steadfast; and whose hand it was that always supported me to stick to one point of view and not the other. Right now people have come here from all sides but there was a time when just a handful of them were initiated into the Jamā'at. The question is, why, for the sake of unity among the members of the Jamā'at, did I not retreat from my position and let this so-called unity stay intact? To answer this, today I would like to explain what has always kept me strong and resolute in my stance. But before I speak on that, I would like to touch on a few other things.

Misunderstandings About Khilāfat

Does a Khalīfah have to be Divinely Appointed or a Ruler?

One objection made in this regard by some people is that only a person who is either a king or is directly appointed by God can be a

Khalīfah. Such people ask me, 'Who are you? Are you a king'? I say, 'No.' 'Have you been directly appointed by God?' I say, 'No.' 'How can you be the *Khalīfah* then?', they ask me. They imagine that it is compulsory for the *Khalīfah* to be either a king or directly appointed by God. In fact, those who raise this objection have not pondered over the word '*Khalīfah*' at all. Their point of view in this regard is no different than that of a person who goes to the shop of a tailor and finds that a young trainee is addressing his master as '*Khalīfah*'. Having heard this, he comes out of the shop and proclaims that '*Khalīfah*' is a title to be used only for a tailor. Similar is the condition of a person who, having visited a school, finds that students use the title of '*Khalīfah*' for their monitor [in the past *Khalīfah* was the title used for the student who monitored a class] and then proclaims that a *Khalīfah* is only he who monitors a class of school boys. Hence, one who does not monitor the students cannot be a *Khalīfah*, because to his poor intellect being a *Khalīfah* is conditional upon monitoring some students.

Similar is the case of a person who, having observed that God made a *Khalīfah* and ordered the angels to prostrate before him, starts inferring that *Khalīfah* can only be he to whom the angels are ordered to prostrate. Otherwise, he concludes, no other person can be a *Khalīfah*. Similar is the situation of the person who observes that the *Khulafā'* of the Holy Prophet[sa] had kingdoms and sovereign governments, and therefore concludes that only a person who has a kingdom can be a *Khalīfah* and no other person should be addressed as *Khalīfah*, for being a *Khalīfah* requires one to have a kingdom. Those who say this are absolutely unaware of what the word *Khalīfah* stands for. In fact, the word signifies the one who is called someone's successor and who should succeed his predecessor's work for all practical purposes. If someone is a tailor, then the person doing the same work after him is his *Khalīfah*, and if a student takes up the task of conducting a class in the absence of his teacher, that student will be called the *Khalīfah* of the teacher. Likewise, one who succeeds the work of a Prophet is a *Khalīfah* of that Prophet. If God grants kingdom to His Prophet, his *Khalīfah* will also be entitled to it and God will surely vouchsafe the kingdom upon him. But if the Prophet happens to be without a kingdom, from where will it come for his *Khalīfah*? Because God had granted both the worldly and spiritual kingdoms to the Holy Prophet[sa], his *Khulafā'* too were granted both of these bounties. But now, as God has not vouchsafed a worldly kingdom upon the Promised Messiah[as], with whom should his *Khalīfah* fight to have one? Those who raise this objection have not duly reflected upon the word '*Khalīfah*'. Would not such a person be considered a fool who, having seen people here wearing turbans, caps and clothes, should note down with him that humans beings are only classified as those who wear turbans, caps and clothes of a specific type? Then when he goes out and finds that people are not dressed as he had thought they should be, he starts proclaiming that the people he saw were not human beings since human beings have a specific dress code? What do you think of such a person? He is definitely a credulous fool. Similarly, if someone, having seen the *Khulafā'* of certain Prophets concludes that *Khulafā'* can only be of a particular kind and none other; can his statement be acceptable to any sane person? No, never! Such a person should rather ponder over the word '*Khalīfah*' and reflect upon its meanings. In this age, too, people have misunderstood the word '*Khalīfah*' on account of their being ignorant of the Arabic language. According to the Arabic language, *Khalīfah* is he:

1. who succeeds someone,
2. who is succeeded by someone, and
3. who issues commands and orders and gets them executed.

In addition to this, *Khulafā'* are of two types. The first type are those who succeed someone after his death. Second are those who work as subordinates to someone during his lifetime; for example, a viceroy who serves as *Khalīfah* to the king. Now, should someone say that since the viceroy has nothing to do with religion, he cannot be a *Khalīfah* to the king, he would certainly be in error, because the king of whom the viceroy happens to be a *Khalīfah* is possessed of only a worldly government. The viceroy is a *Khalīfah* to the king only in matters related to the worldly government, and not in matters of religion. This is a clear-cut argument which some people have failed to understand, or perhaps they simply do not want to understand it.

Resemblance with Earlier Khilāfats

Again, such people also raise the objection that since the Promised Messiah[as] came in the image of the Messiah of the Israelites, his *Khulafā'* should also resemble the *Khulafā'* of the Messiah of the Israelites. But should we accept their point of view, we will have to contend that there should not be any *Khulafā'* after the Promised

Messiah[as] because there is no proof of any successors after the Messiah of the Israelites. So, in the first place, this argument of theirs is a totally invalid. We believe that Jesus did not die on the cross, and that he lived for almost 80 years after the crucifixion. The Gospel, which is devoid of any mention of *Khilāfat* after him, is in fact a history of his lifetime only up to the time of the crucifixion. Therefore, how can one, merely by reading the Gospel, come to know whether any *Khilāfat* had ever succeeded Jesus, peace be upon him? To believe this is like someone putting forth *Barāhīn-e-Aḥmadiyya*, a book of the Promised Messiah[as], and arguing that there is no mention of any *Khilāfat* or anyone being a *Khalīfah* after the Promised Messiah[as] which proves that he was not succeeded by a *Khalīfah*. Similarly, how can anybody find some *Khalīfah* of the Prophet Jesus from the Gospel when it narrates his life history only up to 33 years of his age, whereas we know from the sayings of the Holy Prophet[sa] that Prophet Jesus lived for 120 years. Considering that Jesus remained alive after the 33 years of his biblical life, how can one come to know about his successors merely by reading the Gospel? Should anyone suggest that even after his death at the age of 120, there is no mention of a *Khalīfah*, then our point of view is that if someone brings us the history of Jesus' life after the first 30 years, we would also be obliged to produce the names of his *Khulafā'*? Since the history of the life of Jesus regarding his later years is not available, it is simply ridiculous to argue about the existence of his *Khulafā'*. Someone might argue that crucifixion and migrating from one's country is like suffering death, and the Promised Messiah[as] has written in *al-Waṣiyyat*, that 'the same had happened to the Prophet Jesus as well'—i.e., he was succeeded by a *Khalīfah*—and then ask us mention the name of his *Khalīfah*. It would be a fair comment, and we can make allowance for that. But, this objection in fact proves that these people have not even pondered over the Gospel. This particular subject has been discussed by the Gospel in the same way as it has been laid down by the Promised Messiah[as] in *al-Waṣiyyat*, and just as the concept of *Khilāfat* and the Anjuman was mentioned in *al-Waṣiyyat*, it has also been mentioned in the Gospel. Jesus' coming to see his disciples after the crucifixion and his decision to move to Kashmir has been mentioned in John, chapter 21 thus:

> So when they had eaten breakfast, Jesus said to Simon Peter, 'Simon, son of Jonah, do you love Me more than these?' He said to Him, 'Yes, Lord; You know that I love You.' He said to him, 'Feed My lambs.' He said to him again a second time, 'Simon, son of Jonah, do you love Me?' He said to him, 'Yes, Lord; You know that I love You.' He said to him, 'Tend My sheep.' He said to him the third time, 'Simon, son of Jonah, do you love Me?' Peter was grieved because He said to him the third time, 'Do you love me?' And he said to him, 'Lord, You know all things; you know that I love You.' Jesus said to him, 'Feed My sheep.[5]

Hence, it is clear that Jesus appointed Peter as his successor. In Luke, chapter 9, we find this written about Jesus:

> Then He called His twelve disciples together and gave them power and authority over all demons, and to cure diseases. He sent

---

[5] Verses: 15, 16, 17

> them to preach the kingdom of God and to heal the sick.[6] So they departed and went through the towns, preaching the gospel and healing everywhere.[7]

These verses prove that Jesus had assigned the task of preaching to his disciples, but they also make it clear that he did not give his Jamā'at into the custody of a group of people; rather he only spoke to Peter by saying 'Feed my lamb... Feed my sheep.' However, when it came to initiating people into his fold, Jesus called upon all of his disciples to preach the kingdom of God and heal the sick. Similar instructions have been set out by the Promised Messiah[as] in *al-Waṣiyyat*. However, when he mentioned his *Khulafā'*, he wrote,

> This is the Way of God. And ever since He created man on earth He has always been demonstrating this Divine practice. He helps His Prophets[as] and Messengers[as] and grants them success and predominance, as He says:[8]
>
> كَتَبَ اللّٰهُ لَاَغۡلِبَنَّ اَنَا وَ رُسُلِيۡ ...
>
> And by predominance is meant that as Messengers[as] and Prophets[as] desire that God's *Ḥujjat*[9] is established in the world and no one is able to oppose it, so, in turn, does God demonstrate with powerful

---

6 Verses: 1, 2

7 *Ibid.*, verse 6

8 Allah has decreed: 'Most surely I will prevail, I and My Messengers.' (*Sūrah al-Mujādalah*, 58:22)

9 Literally argument. Here it means Will, Purpose of God.

signs their truthfulness as well as the truth they wish to spread in the world. He lets them sow the seed of it [the truth], but He does not let it come to full fruition at their hands. Rather He causes them to die at such time as apparently forebodes a kind of failure and thereby provides an opportunity for the opponents to laugh at, ridicule, taunt, and reproach the Prophets[as]. And after they have had their fill of ridicule and reproach, He reveals yet another dimension of His Might and creates such means by which the objectives which had to some extent remained incomplete are fully realized. Thus He manifests two kinds of Power. (1) First He shows the Hand of His Power at the hands of His Prophets[as] themselves. (2) Second, when with the death of a Prophet[as], difficulties and problems arise and the enemy feels stronger and thinks that things are in disarray and is convinced that now this Jamā'at will become extinct and even members of the Jamā'at, too, are in a quandary and their backs are broken, and some of the unfortunate ones choose paths that lead to apostasy, then it is that God for the second time shows His Mighty Power and supports and takes care of the shaken Jamā'at. Thus one who remains steadfast till the end witnesses this miracle of God. This is what happened at the time of Ḥaḍrat Abū Bakr Ṣiddīq[ra], when the demise of the Holy Prophet[sa] was considered untimely and many an ignorant Bedouin turned apostate. The Companions[ra] of the Holy Prophet[sa], too, stricken with grief, became like those who lose their senses. Then Allah raised Abū Bakr Ṣiddīq[ra] and showed for the second time the manifestation of His Power and saved

Islam, just when it was about to fall, and fulfilled the promise which was spelled out in the verse:[10]

...وَلَيُمَكِّنَنَّ لَهُمْ دِيْنَهُمُ الَّذِى ارْتَضٰى لَهُمْ
وَلَيُبَدِّلَنَّهُمْ مِّنْۢ بَعْدِ خَوْفِهِمْ اَمْنًا ...

That is, after the fear We shall firmly re-establish them. That is also what happened at the time of Moses[as], when he died on his way from Egypt to Canaan before taking the Israelites to the intended destination in accordance with the promise. At his death Israelites were plunged into deep mourning. It is written in Torah that with the grief at this untimely death and sudden departure of Moses[as], the Israelites wept for forty days.[11] The same happened with Christ[as]. At the time of the incident of Crucifixion all his disciples scattered and even one of them apostatized. (*al-Waṣiyyat*, p. 6–7, Islam International Publication, printed 2005)

The Promised Messiah[as] has prescribed the same method for saving a Jamā'at from disintegration which was practised after the death of the Holy Prophet[sa], Prophet Moses[as] and Prophet Jesus[as], i.e., that there came successors after them. But as far as the propagation of faith is concerned, the Promised Messiah[as] has said:

---

[10] And that He will surely establish for them their religion which He has chosen for them; and that He will surely give them in exchange security and peace after their fear. (*Sūrah an-Nūr*, 24:56)

[11] Deuteronomy chapter 34 verse 8. Note: Some editions mention 30 instead of 40 days.

> Let the righteous persons of the Jamā'at who have pure souls accept *bai'at* in my name God Almighty desires to draw all those who live in various habitations of the world, be it Europe or Asia, and who have virtuous nature, to the Unity of God and unite His servants under one Faith. This indeed is the purpose of God for which I have been sent to the world. You, too, therefore should pursue this end, but with kindness, moral probity and fervent prayers. And till that time when someone inspired by God with the Holy Spirit is raised by Him, all of you should work in harmony with one another. (*al-Waṣiyyat*, p. 8, Islam International Publication, printed 2005)

The writings of Jesus, therefore, are similar to those of the Promised Messiah[as] for his Jamā'at. However, Jesus had specifically mentioned Peter's name and had put his sheep (disciples) into his care, but because the faith of the Messiah of Muhammad, peace be upon him, was stronger than Jesus Christ, he did not name any specific person and put the matter into God's hands that He should raise whosoever He may please. Besides, he ordered a group of the faithful to, 'Take oath of allegiance from people in my name'. We believe that every Ahmadi is under the obligation to follow this command. Hence, as Jesus had put his Jamā'at into Peter's care, the Promised Messiah[as] too has ordered his Jamā'at to give themselves up under the command of a single person; and as Jesus had commanded his disciples to propagate their religion, similarly, the Promised Messiah[as] commanded some from among his Jamā'at to take oaths of allegiance from others.

Pertinent Incidents

I will now narrate a few incidents to you. Those who are sitting here should attentively listen to me and convey my words to those who are not present here at this time.

Discussions About the Need for a Khalīfah

When Ḥaḍrat Khalīfatul-Masīḥ I[ra] became seriously ill, I pondered over the disagreement I had with a faction of the Jamā'at, and reflected upon the matter a great deal. Having come to realize that the faction had disagreements upon certain tenets, I thought that the people belonging to the other group would never accept our point of view, so it might be better if we concede to their point of view. Having considered the matter in depth, I thought of a person and decided to take oath of allegiance at his hand in case of any disagreement and hoped that those who accompanied me at that time would also join me. I thought my doing so would help establish unity and harmony among the members of the Jamā'at. The day Khalīfatul-Masīḥ I[ra] passed away the same person met me in the early part of the day and joined me in walking. He said that the time had not yet come to debate about the *Khalīfah*, and that the issue would be resolved when those who were coming from outside would all have arrived. I said that they would be here in a matter of just a couple of days. So, I told him, the issue must be resolved when they have all arrived. His answer was, 'let things be as they are for some seven or eight months. Then we would see to the matter. Why show such urgency about it?' I said, 'should you ask my opinion, I would say the issue of *Khilāfat* is indeed a very important one, and that it should be resolved as early as possible'. I then asked him if he could specifically mention even a single project during the lifetime of Ḥaḍrat Khalīfatul-Masīḥ I[ra] that would have remained incomplete if he were not in his position as *Khulafā'*, and for which he had to be appointed as the *Khalīfah*? I told him that if Khalīfatul-Masīḥ I[ra] was needed even in times when there was no crisis, then he had to realize that a *Khalīfah* is always needed and is needed even today.

I told him that the function of a *Khalīfah* was to rectify flaws in the Jamā'at whenever they emerged, and that his job was not to work like a machine which continues working unstopped. I said, 'Maybe you are not aware that the Jamā'at can suffer some discord the very day we are in. In that case, who is going to adjudicate the matter'? I assured him that we would not initiate any problem with regard to the issue of *Khilāfat*, and asked him to even suggest some suitable person for the job. I rather went as far as saying that I was ready to take *bai'at* at the person's hand, and that there were some other people also who were close to me. So, they too would get initiated. Similarly, there were a few, I told him, who enjoyed good relations with that person, so they too would be willing to take *bai'at* at his hand. I told him the matter would thus be settled.

Then I said that the debate should not be whether there should be a *Khalīfah*, but there can be a discussion of who the *Khalīfah* should be. At that time, I reiterated that he should nominate some person from among his own friends, and that I would be ready to pledge allegiance to any such person, but I made it clear that I would never accept the notion that a *Khalīfah* was not needed. I said that even if all the people happened to abandon their belief and only a few were to support my point of view that there should be a *Khalīfah*, we would get initiated into someone's *bai'at*, and choose someone as our *Khalīfah*. But we would never accept that a *Khalīfah* was not needed. I said that it could be anyone; no matter whether the person considered non-Aḥmadīs to be disbelievers or not; whether he considered it lawful or unlawful to pray behind them; whether he liked to have relations with them or not; at any cost, there must be a *Khalīfah* so that the unity among the members of the Jamā'at remain unaffected. I said that we were ready to get initiated into such person's *bai'at*.

However, the discussion remained inconclusive at that time. So, it was thought appropriate to discuss the matter once again for further consideration. Also, it was proposed that a few more people should be included to talk things over. Five or six people turned up the next day to discuss the matter. What followed was a lengthy debate concerning the point whether there was any need of a *Khalīfah*. But after a lengthy debate and discussion when there was not much time left, I said that we were left with only one choice, i.e., those who thought a *Khalīfah* was really needed should get initiated into someone's *bai'at* after electing him as their leader. We would gather like-minded people at one place and ask for their advice, and tell those who did not believe in the need of a *Khalīfah* to keep away from us, so that there was no trouble. After that we came here into the Nūr Mosque. They too came along. What followed was as God had willed. Those sitting beside me at that time know very well about my feelings at that time. If I had already made up my mind about following some illicit plan, I would surely have memorized the words of *bai'at*. Instead, I had to ask someone to read them for me. Is that how clever schemes are hatched?

Incident at the Nūr Mosque

One more objection made by these people is that someone had stood up to make a speech [in the Nūr Mosque], but he was not allowed and was asked to sit down. In their opinion, this caused the person too much of humiliation. My point is that there would have been no harm at all even if he had been beaten on the spot. The reason being that he failed to recognize the need of a *Khalīfah* appointed by God. The person must have later learnt that it was in fact Nurud-Dīn, the Khalīfatul-Masīḥ I[ra], who had safeguarded his honour. As soon as he closed his eyes from the world, this man suffered disrepute. This proves that the need for a *Khalīfah* is always urgent. He is not needed seven or eight months after the demise of the earlier *Khalīfah*. As for me, at that time, I really did not know who had stood up to make the speech. Having come out of the mosque, someone told me that there was a man who said that Qadian was a hospital and all who lived there were sick. I asked him why the person had made such a comment. He replied that it was because when Maulavī Muhammad Ali stood up to speak, he was denied permission to do so, and that this caused him [Maulavī Muhammad Ali] a lot of embarrassment. That was the moment when I really came to know about the incident. Moreover, even if I had come to know about it at the time it was taking place, what right did I have to stop someone from preventing them from speaking on the subject? And what was the relationship of the people with me at that time that they would have paid any attention to what I might possibly have said. In fact, no one had yet been chosen as Imam by then.

Maulavi Muhammad Ali's Decision to Leave Qadian

Then there was another incident. I heard that Maulavī Muhammad Ali was preparing to leave Qadian. I wrote to him that I had heard that he wanted to leave and asked him why he was doing so. I requested him to write back to me about the problem he was facing. Having written the message, I gave it to Doctor Khalifah Rashidud-Din so as to take it to him [Muhammad Ali]. I did not send it through some servant lest he should say that he suffered humiliation because of my sending it through some servant of mine. I also asked Doctor Ṣāḥib to enquire of him why he was leaving, and to convey to him that if he was not feeling comfortable, it was my responsibility to help him. The answer he gave was how could he leave Qadian and go somewhere else. He said that I was personally aware of his having taken the permission to leave, and that he simply intended to avail his holidays. In the end of his reply he also mentioned that another reason why he wanted to leave was that there were people who were a bit too agitated against him, hence, he thought it appropriate to go away for a few days so that their agitation may recede, and lest someone from among the Pathans should feel tempted to attack him. Anyway, much emphasis was placed in his letter on the point that there was simply no need for him to leave Qadian and go somewhere else, and that he was going away solely with the intent of spending his holidays.

Thereafter, I personally went to see him at his home. Nawwāb Ṣāḥib was also with me. Having arrived at his place, initially there was some discussion about some peripheral matters. The translation he was doing of the Holy Quran was also discussed. Then, Dr. Ṣāḥib, in order to shift the emphasis of discussion to the point at issue, told him that the purpose of my personally visiting him was to discuss the contents of the letter he had written to me. Upon hearing these words Maulavī Ṣāḥib reacted in a way which made us feel that he wanted to put us off. I am not sure if he really intended to do so but he should have at least given some regard to the fact that though he and his fellows had dissented, there was still a section of the Jamā'at which had chosen me as their Imam. What actually happened was that there was a man called Bagga. Maulavī Ṣāḥib found him standing outside his bungalow and started chatting with him saying, 'Come here, Mian Bagga! When did you come back from Lahore?' This was followed by indulging in a lengthy talk with him about some petty matters. Having seen this, we stood up and came back. What I understood from Maulavī Muhammad Ali's behaviour was that he simply didn't want to discuss the matter. Only God knows whether this was really how he intended to behave, but since those who accompanied me also reached the same conclusion, we left immediately.

Steps to Maintain Unity

In addition to personally visiting him, I also thought of taking certain other steps to keep the people united and in harmony with each other. When the condition of Ḥaḍrat Khalīfatul-Masīḥ became critical, and I came to know that some people were labelling me as a mischief monger, I decided to leave Qadian and return only when the matter was settled once for all. Having returned from Nawwāb Ṣāḥib's bungalow where Ḥaḍrat Khalīfatul-Masīḥ was taking bed rest, I went into my drawing room and offered prayer. I beseeched Allah the Almighty, 'O my Lord! If I am the bone of contention, cause me to die, or enable me to stay away from Qadian for a few days.' After the prayer, I returned to Nawwāb Ṣāḥib's mansion. It was there that God inspired my heart with the words: 'We shall take care. You must not leave here.'

I have already sworn once, but here again I swear by the Being in whose hand my life is, and to whom belongs this house [mosque], and I swear by Him whose rule extends to the heavens and the earth and to swear falsely in whose name makes one accursed and whose curse is such as leaves no liar unpunished, that I have never ever begged anyone to make any attempts to get me elected as *Khalīfah*, neither have I ever beseeched God to appoint me as *Khalīfah*. But when Allah the Almighty Himself chose me for this task, how could I dislike it? Should some friend of yours give you some gift but later find out that you threw his gift into the drain, do you think this act of yours would please him? Besides, do you think it would be appropriate to do so? No, never! Hence, when God showers His bounty on someone, who can stop him from taking it? When one does not refuse to accept the gifts of worldly friends—rather greatly regards them and holds them in high esteem—how can I turn down the bounty of God that has been vouchsafed upon me by Him? Those who rejected God's bounties always met horrible ends. The people of Moses accompanied Moses all the way to Mount Sinai. God called upon them to come there so as to speak with them. But when an earthquake hit them there, they were frightened and said that they did not want to hear the words of God, and returned to their homes. God, because of their rejecting His bounty, punished them by declaring that no law-bearing Prophet would ever be raised from among them; He said that, on the contrary, he would be raised from among their brethren. Hence, when I had already seen how God punished those who rejected His bounty, how could I refuse to accept it? I firmly believed that God, who had chosen me for this task, would Himself strengthen my hands, and would bestow steadfastness and perseverance upon me. Hence, had even those who acknowledged my *Khilāfat* immediately turned apostate and had I been left with not even a single follower and had the whole world become my enemy and had become thirsty for my life – that is maximum they would have been able to do – for even then I would have refused to budge and would have never thought of turning down God's blessing, for this mistake, once made, brings horrible consequences.

Dire Consequences of Abandoning the Robe of Khilāfat

Imam Hasan[ra] made the same mistake, the consequences of which were indeed grave. However, he made this mistake on account of a specific view of his, i.e., he believed that a son should not inherit *Khilāfat* from his father. Ḥaḍrat Umar[ra] also held the same view and I am also of the same opinion. It was for this reason that Ḥaḍrat Umar[ra], regarding the election of the *Khalīfah* after him, said that though his son should be consulted, he would not be entitled to be elected as *Khalīfah*. Ḥaḍrat Ali[ra] appointed his son, Imam Hasan[ra] as *Khalīfah* after him. Of course, he did this with the best of intentions, for there was no other person who could be chosen as *Khalīfah* and who was truly worthy of the seat of *Khilāfat*. It seems as if Ḥaḍrat Hasan[ra] held the same view as Ḥaḍrat

Umar[ra], i.e., a son should not inherit *Khilāfat* from his father. That is why he later became reconciled with Mu'awiya[ra], which consequently resulted in the martyrdom of Imam Husain[ra] and many of his family members. Once Imam Hasan[ra] refused to accept the Divine bounty of *Khilāfat*, God decided that no one from amongst them should ever be granted this blessing again. Hence, since then, no Sayyed has ever become a king. They have ruled only small and insignificant territories; they were never granted true kingship and *Khilāfat*. Imam Hasan[ra] turned down God's bounty, an act which resulted in horrible consequences. Therefore, it is not a trivial matter to reject God's bounties that He wishes to bestow upon His servants.

Remember that he who calls upon me to abandon the robe of *Khilāfat* has not at all partaken of true recognition of God and is unable to understand the wisdom behind His acts. Such an ignorant person has no idea of the consequences of such an act. Therefore, like Ḥaḍrat Usman[ra], I too have declared that I would never take off the robe that has been bestowed upon me by God Himself. I shall never take it off even if the whole world were bent upon snatching it from me. Therefore, whether someone joins me or not, I will continue to march forward. God the Exalted has revealed to me that there would be ordeals and trials, but the end would be good. Therefore, anyone who dares may come forward to oppose me. God willing, I will prevail. It does not matter who dares to come out and have a contest with me.

There are things which only I can tell. Nobody knows how heavy is the weight of the responsibility that I have been asked to bear. There are days when I feel that I would die even before sunset. On such occasions, I say to myself 'I should continue to work so long as I am living and after my demise God will raise someone else in my place. My worry about the work that God has assigned to me will last only until the time I am living'. Therefore, I worry least about what would happen after I have passed away. This Movement has been initiated by God Almighty, so He Himself will look after it.

Has Khilāfat Assumed a Hereditary Characteristic?

As for the statement of ignorant people who say that *Khilāfat* has now become a succession by heredity, I declare by God that I do not at all consider it lawful that a son should inherit *Khilāfat* from his father. However, it would be a different matter if God Himself appointed someone as *Khalīfah* after his father. Otherwise, like Ḥaḍrat Umar[ra], I am of the opinion that a son should not inherit *Khilāfat* from his father.

Again, they assert that the six year period [of the *Khilāfat* of Ḥaḍrat Khalīfatul-Masīḥ I[ra]] does not constitute a binding precedent, and that we should focus instead, on the words of *al-Waṣiyyat*. I say, let alone the six years that you refer to, we should readily sacrifice all of the practices during the twelve hundred years that elapsed between the demise of the Holy Prophet[sa] and the commissioning of the Promised Messiah[as]. But never in history have we ever come across an example where the Jamā'at of a Prophet, after his demise, was united upon a false creed. But in our case, not even a single day had passed when the Jamā'at of the Promised

Messiah[as] agreed upon establishing the institution of *Khilāfat*. Was this a consensus on falsehood, God forbid? No, never!

Many a time they ask: 'Do you consider us to be hypocrites?' My answer to them is that we do not call them hypocrites, except for those whose hearts have become absolutely devoid of truthfulness and who, on their own, confess that they are hypocrites.

Again, if we accept—according to what they claim—that only one-twentieth of the Jamā'at has initiated at my hand by now, they must not forget that after the demise of the Promised Messiah[as] the whole Jamā'at was initiated at the hand of one *Khalīfah*. They may argue that the Jamā'at had consensus on falsehood; but in that case, they would fail to find a precedent of such a consensus in the past history.

The strongest arguments that the Promised Messiah[as] has given to prove the death of Jesus[as] was the verse:[12]

...فَلَمَّا تَوَفَّيْتَنِيْ كُنْتَ اَنْتَ الرَّقِيْبَ عَلَيْهِمْ...

The Promised Messiah[as] said that the second most valid argument in this respect was the consensus of the companions of the Holy Prophet[sa]. But, alas, today it is asserted by these people that after the Promised Messiah[as] passed away, the consensus reached by the Jamā'at and held for six long years, had been on falsehood – God forbid. This might have been possible if those indulging in such an error had not seen the Promised Messiah[as] or had been those who had never benefited from his blessed company; but it is simply

[12] But since You caused me to die, You have been the Watcher over them. (*Sūrah al-Mā'idah*, 5:118)

impossible for the companions of the Promised Messiah[as] to make such a blunder. If his companions were to make such mistakes, then of what benefit was his advent?

There is no doubt that there are some among us who are weak of faith, but was there not a whole group of hypocrites living at the time of the Holy Prophet[sa]? Moreover, why was it that a few who always remained among the party of the Companions of the Holy Prophet[sa] are not remembered with the salutation "May Allah be pleased with them". As a matter of fact, they are not even counted among the Companions of the Prophet[sa] The only reason is that they were hypocrites. They paid lip service to the Holy Prophet[sa], whereas, at heart, they were devoid of true faith. The same is our stance now. We will call all those who have been sincerely following the commands of the Promised Messiah[as] both in the past and the present the Companions of the Promised Messiah[as]; but we will not bestow this title on those who will not follow the teachings of the Promised Messiah[as]. Did Abdullah bin Ubayy not live in the company of the Holy Prophet[sa], and did he not pass his time among the Companions? Yet, he is not counted as one of the Companions. This is because he was a hypocrite. Similarly, if a person from among the companions of the Promised Messiah[as] falls into error, it would be his own fault. It is impossible to believe that just by living in the company of the Promised Messiah[as] for some time one can become secure from the harm which one may invite upon himself as a result of his own mistakes.

I reiterate that we are not alone in presuming that after the demise of the Promised Messiah[as] the Jamā'at did not go astray as a whole. The fact is that the Promised Messiah[as] had received this revelation long before his demise:

سپردم بتو مایۂ خویش را ٭ تو دانی حساب کم و بیش را

I have committed all my capital to you. You know all about profit and loss. (*Tadhkirah*, second English Edition p. 1051, published by Islam International Publications, 2009)

The Promised Messiah[as], therefore, laid all his assets at God's threshold, so that God Himself took care of them. God told him to entrust his Jamā'at to Him, and that He Himself would protect it. Now, if we were to accept the stance of the disbelievers of *Khilāfat*, then what kind of protection was provided to the Jamā'at when God allowed their very first consensus to be on falsehood? The Promised Messiah[as] had committed his Jamā'at to God. God entrusted it to Nurud-Dīn, an act which some, God forbid, dare say was committed in sheer falsehood. I dare ask these people: was God not capable of saving His Jamā'at from Nurud-Dīn if that was the necessary step to protect them against going astray? Indeed He was! Yet, He never did that. This act of God, therefore, proves that the consensus of the Jamā'at was not on falsehood; rather, it was exactly in accordance with divine Will.

It was for these reasons that I remained firm in my stance. Moreover, there are certain other reasons and they are more important than the ones I have mentioned earlier. I have done nothing out of my own presumption in such matters; instead, I always believed that whatever happened was decreed by God. These reasons are such that they do not allow me to retreat from my position. They are not a testimony from this world, but from the heavens; and they are not from the realm of men, but are from God Almighty Himself. So how can I retreat from my position? Even if the whole world accuses me of being wrong in my stance, I would tell them that it is in fact they who are in the wrong and only that which is conveyed by God is true; for He is the Most Truthful of all those who speak the truth.

Path of Reconciliation

There are people who suggest reconciliation between the two parties. I would like to ask them if in that case the other party would abandon their belief that there should be no *Khalīfah*. Or will we consequently renounce our own belief that there must be a *Khalīfah*? If none of us are going to abandon our belief, then the proposed reconciliation would result in a grouping of people who hold contradictory beliefs, and consider the beliefs of each other to be extremely harmful for the Jamā'at. Will such a grouping result in harmony or further discord? Yet, **I am ready for reconciliation, and I am the son of the one who was called 'The Prince of Peace'.** However, I cannot accept a reconciliation that destroys the faith; but I am more eager than everybody else for a reconciliation based on firm adherence to the truth.

I deeply appreciate the parable of Jesus which is recorded in Luke, chapter 15. It says:

> A certain man had two sons. And younger of them said to his father, 'Father, give me the portion of goods that falls to me.' So he divided to them his livelihood. And not many days after, the younger son gathered all together, journeyed to a far country, and there wasted his possessions with prodigal living. But when he had

spent all, there arose a severe famine in that land and he began to be in want. Then he went and joined himself to a citizen of that country, and he sent him into his fields to feed swine. And he would gladly have filled his stomach with the pods that the swine ate, and no one gave him anything. But when he came to himself, he said, 'How many of my father's hired servants have bread enough and to spare, and I perish with hunger! I will arise and go to my father and will say to him, 'Father, I have sinned against heaven and before you, and I am no longer worthy to be called your son. Make me like one of your hired servants.' And he arose and came to his father. But when he was still a great way off, his father saw him and had compassion, and ran and fell on his neck and kissed him. And the son said to him, 'Father, I have sinned against heaven and in your sight, and am no longer worthy to be called your son.' But the father said to his servants, 'Bring out the best robe and put it on him, and put a ring on his hand and sandals on his feet. And bring the fatted calf here and kill it, and let us eat and be merry; for this my son was dead and is alive again; he was lost and is found. And they began to be merry. Now, his older son was in the field. And as he came and drew near to the house, he heard music and dancing. So he called one of the servants and asked what these things meant. And he said to him, 'Your brother has come, and because he has received him safe and sound, your father has killed the fatted calf.' But he was angry and would not go in. Therefore, his father came out and pleaded with him. So, he answered and said to his father, 'Lo, these many years I have been serving you; I never transgressed your commandment at any time; and yet you never gave me a young goat that I might make merry with my friends. But as soon as this son of yours came,

> who has devoured your livelihood with harlots; you killed the fatted calf for him. And he said to him, 'Son, you are always with me, and all that I have is yours. It was right that we should make merry and be glad, for your brother was dead and is alive again, and was lost and is found.'

I have a lot of patience and fortitude. If someone comes repenting, I will be happier for him than I am for those who pledged their allegiance to me on the first day of my *Khilāfat*. The reason is that the latter were never lost. But the aforesaid was lost and would be found again. It pleases a father to look at his sons, but the happiness a father feels about his son who suffers a serious illness and recovers is beyond recount. I do not appreciate reconciliation which has traces of hypocrisy. Anyone who extends his hand for reconciliation after washing his heart clean and correcting his mistakes will find that I am readier than him for reconciliation.

No Hypocritical Appeasement

I now wish to make another point. Those who wish to attain a hypocritical reconciliation should remember that it will never happen, for whatever has happened in recent days, has happened in accordance with the divine Will. Those wishing to join us will continue to join us and will be given the same position and respect as they enjoyed before. Whatever was destined has come to pass. No man was strong or capable enough to prevent it from happening. God had foretold the Promised Messiah[as] about this impending ordeal long ago. Those with a weak heart ask me what would happen next. Such people think that the Ahmadiyya Movement will come to an end. To me such ordeals cannot cause a movement to die. Instead, they give the Movement a new life. Blessed is he who understands this salient point. The number of God's beloveds grows even further when they are caused to suffer under divine Will. Haven't you ever observed a gardener? When he cuts off some branches of a tree, the tree begins to develop even more shoots. Similarly, God has cut off certain branches of the Ahmadiyya Movement—not to cause it to be dried and withered, but to cause it to thrive even more than before. Therefore, never think that this trial would make people believe that the very Movement is false, because the trial is, in fact, showing the opposite. It is proving that the prophecies of the Promised Messiah[as] have been fulfilled. Should a Prophet fall ill and his opponents become glad that now the Prophet would die, whereas the Prophet shows them a revelation of his and declares his illness to be a sign of his truth, making it known to his opponents that he had already been informed by God about his illness and that he would recover from it—in such a case, the incident of his falling ill would not blemish the claim of his Prophethood at all; rather, it would strengthen his claim further. Hence, when we had been foretold about this ordeal, it did not hinder our progress in any way. In fact, through this trial, God has vouchsafed to us the swords of strong and incontrovertible arguments, so that we can continue to hasten our enemies to their demise.

Conflict was Bound to Occur

This conflict was bound to happen, please consider:

(1) The Promised Messiah[as] had related a dream of his on December 7, 1892. He narrated it thus:

> I saw another dream on December 7, 1892 that I had become Ḥaḍrat Ali, may Allah honour his face; meaning that in my dream I felt as if I was the very same as him. It is one of the wonders of a dream that sometimes a person feels that he is someone else and in that way I felt at the time that I was Ali Murtada and the situation was that a group[13] of Khawārij was opposing my *Khilāfat*, that is to say, they wished to obstruct my becoming *Khalīfah* and were creating mischief for that purpose. Then I saw the Holy Prophet, on whom be peace and blessings of Allah, close to me and he said with kindness and affection:
>
> يَا عَلِيُّ دَعْهُمْ وَأَنْصَارَهُمْ وَزِرَاعَتَهُمْ
>
> **O Ali! Stay away from them, their helpers, and their harvest. Leave them and turn away from them.**
>
> I found that the Holy Prophet, may the peace and blessings of Allah be upon him, advised me to be steadfast in the midst of that trial and to refrain from getting involved with those people. He told me that I was in the right, but that it would be better not to address them. (*Ā'īna-e-Kamālāt-e-Islām*, pp. 218–219 footnote, *Rūḥānī Khazā'in*, vol. 5, pp. 218–219 footnote, See also

---

[13] This shows that the *Khilāfat* that would be established after the Promised Messiah[as] would be opposed by a community which will try to create disorder.

Tadhkirah, second English Edition p. 271, published by Islam International Publications, 2009)

In this dream, it was revealed to the Promised Messiah[as] that people would oppose his *Khilāfat* and that they would try to create problems for him, but that the Promised Messiah[as] would have to remain steadfast. The Promised Messiah[as] interpreted this dream to mean that people would reject him, but divine Words contain manifold meanings. Take, for example, the revelation

شا تان تذ بحان

The Promised Messiah[as] had interpreted his revelation differently in the beginning, but later he applied it to [the martyrdoms of] Sayyed Abdul-Latif Shaheed and Maulavī Abdur-Rahman. Both the interpretations were correct.

Hence, one meaning of the dream about Ḥaḍrat Ali[ra] was that people would oppose the Promised Messiah[as], and the other which is clearly reflected in the words of the dream was that the *Khilāfat* that would succeed the Promised Messiah[as] would also be opposed by a large number of people, and that such people would try to create great uproar. Hence, how could this prophecy have come true if there had not been a group of people who rejected the *Khilāfat* after the Promised Messiah[as]?

(2) People say that those who have declared *Khilāfat* to be unlawful are quite influential. We do accept that they are, but the Promised Messiah[as] was writing about the same kind of people when he wrote:

> Anyone who does not completely commit his life, wealth, and honour in this way, I say it very truly that in the sight of God he has not yet been initiated. On the contrary, I have observed that many of those who outwardly enter into the covenant of *bai'at* with me are still not perfect in the trait of thinking well. Like a weak child, they stumble at every trial. Some unfortunate ones are quickly affected by that which the wicked ones allege and they rush into ill-thinking as a dog rushes towards carrion. Then how can I say that they have truly entered my *bai'at?* From time to time I am given knowledge of these people, but I am not permitted to inform them specifically. **There are many small ones who will be exalted and there are many exalted ones who will be reduced.** Hence, the time is such that everyone needs to be in awe of God and fear Him. (*Barāhīn-e-Aḥmadiyya*, vol. 5, *Rūḥānī Khazā'in*, vol. 21, p. 114)

How could the truth of the Jamā'at be established if what was destined to happen since time immemorial, and about which the Promised Messiah[as] was informed by God time and again, had not come to pass? How could this truth be established if some superior ones had not been made to be inferior ones, and if the Jamā'at which was suppressed and persecuted by its opponents had not grown dramatically in numbers?

(3) Moreover, if the Jamā'at had not become divided into two factions, how the following revelation of the Promised Messiah[as] could have been fulfilled:

خدا دو مسلمان فریق میں سے ایک کا ہوگا۔ پس یہ پھوٹ کا ثمرہ ہے۔

> **God will be with one out of two groups of Muslims. So, this is the consequence of discord.** (*Tadhkirah*, second English Edition p. 945, published by Islam International Publications, 2009)

This revelation clearly pointed out that the Jamā'at would be divided into two groups, but God's support will only be with one of them. Should someone say that by two groups the Allah the Almighty meant Aḥmadīs and Non-Aḥmadīs, and that in the revelation God only meant to inform that He would stand with Aḥmadīs. To this I would respond that in that case the revelation should have been, 'God *is* with one of them' and not that 'God *will be* with one of them', for the words of another revelation are:

إِنِّيْ مَعَكَ وَمَعَ أَهْلِكَ وَمَعَ كُلِّ مَنْ أَحَبَّكَ۔

> **I am with you and with the members of your family and with all those who love you.** (*Tadhkirah*, second English Edition p. 728, published by Islam International Publications, 2009)

This means that God was with Aḥmadīs at the time of that revelation. But the words 'will be' in the revelation under discussion indicate that God will stand by one of the groups against the other at some future time. The words 'will be' in the first revelation, therefore, manifestly prove that the revelation contains the indication of Ahmadiyya Jamā'at getting divided into two groups at some future time. Hence, how could have we seen the fulfilment of this revelation if the present ordeal had not come to pass?

(4) Another claim that the opponents of *Khilāfat* make is that they were among the close fellows and loved ones of the Promised

Messiah[as]. Our response to this is that they are right in making such claims, for there was a time when they certainly enjoyed this privilege. But, have these people forgotten the revelation which the Promised Messiah[as] had narrated early one morning after prayers were requested by Sheikh Rahmatullah in the evening of the day before? The Promised Messiah[as] had said:

> I supplicated earnestly on her behalf and (addressing Sheikh Rahmatullah) for you also. First I received a revelation of which the meanings was somewhat unclear. I do not know about whom it is.
>
> شَرُّ الَّذِيْنَ اَنْعَمْتَ عَلَيْهِمْ
>
> **The Mischief of those on whom you have bestowed your favour.** (*Tadhkirah*, second English Edition p. 723, published by Islam International Publications, 2009)

Therefore, how could the revelation of the Promised Messiah[as] come true today if some of those people upon whom he had showered rewards had not taken part in mischief making? This applies particularly to the person addressing whom the Promised Messiah[as] had narrated this revelation?

(5) There is another revelation dated March 13, 1907. March 13th is the day on which the demise of Ḥaḍrat Khalīfatul-Masīḥ I[ra] took place. A tract was published [against the institution of *Khilāfat*] on the same day from Lahore. How could the following revelation be fulfilled if this tract had not published:

لاہور میں ایک بے شرم ہے۔

There is a shameless one in Lahore. (*Tadhkirah*, second English Edition p. 723, published by Islam International Publications, 2009)

(6) Another objection which these people raise is that initially they were called pious and righteous whereas now they are called evil and disreputable. Our answer to this is that, man can change anytime. Righteous people turn evil and evil people turn righteous. Blessed is he whose end is blessed. Moreover, there was a vision of the Promised Messiah[as] in which he thus spoke to Maulavī Muhammad Ali:

In my dream, I said to Maulavī Muhammad Ali: **You were also righteous and meant well, come and sit down with us.** (*al-Badr*, vol. 3, no. 29, August 1, 1904, p. 4, See also *Tadhkirah*, second English Edition p. 676, published by Islam International Publications, 2009)

Could this have been fulfilled if some of those whom we used to consider righteous and who had wished well for the Jamā'at at some time not been instrumental in creating the trouble now?

(7) Again, in 1909, if someone had not gathered all the members of the Jamā'at at a place in Lahore and forced them to sign and put the impression of their thumbs on a paper which held the view that the successors of the Promised Messiah[as] should have nothing to do with the affairs of the Jamā'at; rather, it was the role of the Anjuman [and not of the *Khalīfah*] to succeed the Promised

Messiah[as]; then how could the vision of the Promised Messiah[as] have been fulfilled in which he had recorded:

> There was a throne laid out on the top of the small mosque and I was sitting on it and with me was Maulavī Nur-ud-Din. One person (whose name need not be disclosed) began to attack us wildly. I said to someone: 'Catch hold of him and expel him from the mosque.' He pushed him down the stairs and he went away running.
>
> Bear in mind that the interpretation of a mosque is the community. (*Tadhkirah*, second English Edition p. 1058, published by Islam International Publications, 2009)

(8) Moreover, if the family of the Promised Messiah[as] had not been attacked during this time of trouble, and the sword of invectives had not been drawn against them, how could the following revelation be fulfilled:

اے میرے اہل بیت! خدا تمہیں شر سے محفوظ رکھے۔

> **O members of my household! May God safeguard you against ill.** (*Tadhkirah*, second English Edition p. 911, 924, published by Islam International Publications, 2009)

After all why would God use these words if the members of the family of the Promised Messiah[as] were not going to face any mischief?

(9) In addition, had their conduct not come under attack, how could the following revelation be fulfilled:

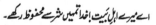

إِنَّمَا يُرِيدُ اللّٰهُ لِيُذْهِبَ عَنْكُمُ الرِّجْسَ أَهْلَ الْبَيْتِ
وَيُطَهِّرَكُمْ تَطْهِيرًا۔

Allah desires to remove from you all uncleanness, O members of the household, and to purify you completely. (*Tadhkirah*, second English Edition p. 911, 923, published by Islam International Publications, 2009)

(10) Again, if some people had not accused Ḥaḍrat Ummul-Mu'mīnīn[ra] [the wife of the Promised Messiah[as]], of hatching plots to seize *Khilāfat* through the canvassing of the female members of the Jamā'at—thus accusing her of forsaking God's will for the attainment of her own desires—then how else could the dream of the Promised Messiah[as] that he saw on March 19, 1907 have come true? This dream has been described by the Promised Messiah[as] as following:

I saw in my dream that my wife said to me:

مَیں نے خدا کی مرضی کے لئے اپنی مرضی چھوڑ دی ہے۔

I have given up my pleasure for the pleasure of God;

And I said to her in reply:

اسی سے تو تم پر حُسن چڑھا ہے

That is why you are glowing with beauty. (*Tadhkirah*, second English Edition p. 934, published by Islam International Publications, 2009)

(11) If my younger brothers, who have not even entered practical life and are still completing their schooling, had not been made the target of attacks because of animosity against me, how else could the dream of the Promised Messiah[as] that he had narrated on August 21, 1906 come true? The dream was thus recorded by the Promised Messiah[as]:

> Last night I saw in my dream that there were such vast numbers of wasps (meaning low enemies) that the whole earth was covered with them and they were greater in number than a locust swarm—so numerous that they virtually covered the ground. Some of them were flying as if they would sting but they did not succeed. I said to my sons, Sharif and Bashir: Recite this verse of the Quran and then blow over your bodies, you will not be harmed. The verse (*Sūrah ash-Shu'arā'*, 26:131) is:
>
> وَإِذَا بَطَشْتُمْ بَطَشْتُمْ جَبَّارِينَ
>
> **And when you lay hands [upon anyone], you lay hands as tyrants.**
>
> Then I woke up. (*Tadhkirah*, second English Edition p. 881, published by Islam International Publications, 2009)

(12) Moreover, I ask the opponents, if the people of Qadian were not to suffer such attacks why would God have said:

ولاتسئم من الناس اصحاب الصفة و ما ادرك مااصحاب الصفة ترى اعينهم تفيض من الدمع

(13) If Lahore had not been destined by God to be made the so-called 'Madinatul-Masīḥ' at this time, why was the Promised Messiah[as] shown in a vision thirty years ago that the name Qadian is written in the middle of the Holy Quran. He was shown that there are three towns recorded in the Holy Quran which are worthy of true respect and reverence: Makkah, Madinah, and Qadian. Moreover, why was the revelation needed?

خدا قادیان میں نازل ہوگا

God will His descend in Qadian. (*Tadhkirah*, second English Edition p. 562, published by Islam International Publications, 2009)

Why was Qadian mentioned so specifically if efforts were not destined to be made to make Lahore to be a city standing rival to Qadian?

(14) Additionally, if no one was to raise objections against the family of the Promised Messiah[as], why would the Promised Messiah[as] have written in 'The Will' that 'God has made an exception in my case and the case of my wife and children. All other men and women must comply with these conditions; and whoever objects will be a hypocrite?'

Hence, it was not possible for anyone to prevent this ordeal from happening, and how could anyone have prevented what had been ordained by God Himself? It was for this reason that it was bound to happen. An infected hand, when beyond treatment, has to be amputated. One who suffers the amputation does not feel happy about it, but it certainly makes him happy to know that the rest of his body is safe after the amputation. Similarly, it grieves us that a part of the Jamā'at has been amputated, but we are also pleased that the remaining part is now secure from the ill-effects of the diseased part.

I now set out the testimonies that God has granted to me regarding this matter. Although I wish that this ordeal had never taken place, but how else could the truth of those revelations and visions that God had shown to the Promised Messiah[as] long before this disorder, be established? As for me, the Promised Messiah's revelations alone were sufficient to guide me. But, my Lord also decided to personally inform me of the impending problems. I am so grateful for this favour of His that I can never do justice to thanking Him adequately. For the benefit of those who are always ready to accept truth, I now wish to relate the testimonies which were vouchsafed to me about the ordeals that struck after the demise of the Promised Messiah[as]. These proofs kept my heart at peace and I felt comfortable that the path I had chosen was the right one. God Almighty also revealed to me such tidings about the future as revived and refreshed my faith in Him.

Further Heavenly Testimonies About Impending Issues of Khilāfat

Every dispute regarding *Khilāfat* revolves around the pivotal point whether the Promised Messiah[as] should be succeeded by a *Khalīfah* or not. Once this issue is settled, the principal issue is settled. Then what remains is just deciding who should succeed him. So, I will begin by putting forth a heavenly testimony regarding this issue, after which I do not think any pious person would dare deny the importance of *Khilāfat*.

First Heavenly Testimony

It was on March 8th, 1907 that I was shown a notebook of revelations in a vision in which I heard someone saying it was the notebook wherein the Promised Messiah[as] recorded his revelations. Thereupon, I found the following words written in the notebook in boldface:

عَسٰۤى اَنْ تَكْرَهُوْا شَيْـًٔا وَّهُوَ خَيْرٌ لَّكُمْ

It may be that you might dislike something, but in reality it may be beneficial for you.

That is, it may be that you dislike a thing, while it is good for you. Then the scene changed and I saw a mosque against whose custodian people had raised a great tumult. At this point, I found myself talking to a person who was from amongst the rioters. While he was still talking to me, I ran away from him saying: 'If I join hands with you, the Prince would be angry with me.' Meanwhile, there appeared a person of fair complexion who told me that there were three categories of those who were associated with the mosque. First, those who only offered prayers in it—they are commendable; second, those who accepted the membership of the Anjuman of the Mosque; and the third, the Mosque's custodian.

I had another dream, at around the same time as this, but that dream need not be mentioned at this point.

Now, should one reflect on these two dreams, he would understand that a year or so before the demise of the Promised Messiah[as] God had already informed me of this disagreement about *Khilāfat*. At that time nobody could have imagined of anything such as *Khilāfat*, and even the Anjuman had not yet become functional. It had come into being just a short time ago and no one could have imagined that this newly born establishment would dare stand as a claimant to the successorship of the Promised Messiah[as]. Rather, it was a time when even the slightest apprehension regarding the demise of the Promised Messiah[as] could not have crossed the minds of any Ahmadi. All of them, despite the publication of The Will, thought that such an incident would take place only after their own death. Who can deny the fact that a lover cannot bear even the thought of the demise of his loved one. The same was the condition of the Ahmadiyya Jamā'at at that time. The fact that Allah the Almighty revealed at such a time every detail about the dispute that was destined to take place regarding *Khilāfat*, and then the literal fulfilment of this prophecy mentioned in those dreams, is such great a sign that no God-fearing person can ever deny the importance of the institution of *Khilāfat*. Is any human being capable of giving tidings of an incident two years prior to its happening, and also predict its occurrence in the face of circumstances when no visible means are apparently available for its fulfilment? And is it possible that his prediction should come true ad verbatim after a period of two years, especially when a whole nation is affected by the outcome of the prediction?

Behold! How clearly had these two visions signified that there was going to be an incident which might seem dangerous, but was to prove beneficial in the end. Hence, the confrontation over *Khilāfat* which started in 1909, apparently seemed to have dangerous consequences, but the greatest benefit that the Jamā'at derived from it was that they came to realize the importance and true status of *Khilāfat*, and Ḥaḍrat Khalīfatul-Masīḥ I[ra] too came to know about the elements that were opposed to *Khilāfat*. This made him emphasize the point repeatedly that a *Khalīfah* is appointed by God alone, and that *Khilāfat* is essential for the Jamā'at to grow and prosper. Such counsels might not have proved beneficial to the mischief-makers, but there are hundreds of people at this time who truly benefited from them and have been saved from losing faith as they had heard a lot on this subject from Ḥaḍrat Khalīfatul-Masīḥ I[ra].

In the second vision, I was shown that there was a mosque and some people had rebelled against its custodian. The mosque, in dreams, is interpreted as the Jamā'at. The vision makes it amply clear that there was going to be a custodian of the mosque (the words custodian and *Khalīfah* are synonyms) and some people would rebel against him, and that someone from among the same people would try to deceive myself as well but I would not fall into their trap and I would make it absolutely clear to them that my joining hands with them would be a source of great displeasure to the Prince. When we look at the revelations of the Promised Messiah[as], we find that he was also called 'The Prince' in some revelations. Hence, the vision meant that those who would join the rebels would earn the displeasure of the Promised Messiah[as], i.e., their action would be against the teachings of the Promised Messiah[as].

This was how the ordeal was foretold, but along with this God also revealed who, among the members of the Jamā'at, would be responsible for creating this discord. Moreover, by setting out that the Prince would be displeased with those who would revolt against the custodian, it is made explicitly clear that the custodian would be in the right and the rebels would be in the wrong. Similarly, by putting forth that the ordinary worshippers would be better as compared to those who belonged to the Anjuman, the vision made it clear that the dispute about *Khilāfat* would not be initiated by the ordinary members of the Jamā'at; rather, it was to be initiated by the group called the Anjuman. Hence, as was proved later, it was the Anjuman that stood up in rebellion. By showing that I would remain uninvolved in this matter, the vision signified that despite being a member of the Anjuman I would not support the mischief makers.

This vision is so clear and obvious that the more one reflects upon it, the more manifest the proof of the glory of God becomes. The truth of *Khilāfat* also becomes so obvious that only those who are ill-fated would dare to deny it.

Should someone observe that the vision, as stated, seems to make these points quite obvious, but what proof do I really have that I actually saw this vision? One may observe that the vision deserves no credit unless I prove to have seen it. I acknowledge the soundness of this argument. Therefore, I put forth the very person of the Promised Messiah[as] to testify to the truth of my claim. People may wonder how the Promised Messiah[as], who passed away so long ago, can come back to the world again and testify in my favour. For their sake, I explain that although the Promised Messiah[as] is not among us now, yet he will testify to the truth of my claim that I had actually seen this vision on 8th March of that year. In fact, I had narrated this vision of mine to the Promised Messiah[as] in the morning of the very next day I had seen it. Having listened to the dream, he became greatly worried and said, 'Mosque is interpreted as the Jamā'at. Maybe some from among the members of my Jamā'at would oppose me. Repeat it so that I can write it down.' I narrated it to him once again and he recorded it in the notebook which he normally used to note down his revelations. First, he put down the date, then wrote 'Vision Seen by Mahmud' and then noted down all the visions. On the pages prior to these three visions and the ones following them are the revelations which the Promised Messiah[as] had himself recorded in it. [At this time, Ḥaḍrat Muṣleḥ-e-Mau'ūd[ra] showed the notebook to the audience] The notebook is still with me and can be produced before every seeker after truth. Those who recognize the handwriting of the Promised Messiah[as] can testify that the contents of the notebook were registered by none other than him. Many revelations over a number of years are recorded in it, and the visions that I have related to you are also recorded in it in the handwriting of the Promised Messiah[as] himself. This is such strong evidence that no true Ahmadi can deny its veracity, for he who denies such clear and explicit signs, will have to deny all other signs.

Having come to know of this vision, everyone can now understand why I am so confident and full of conviction regarding the importance of *Khilāfat*, and why in the face of every ordeal I have been such a strong supporter of the institution of *Khilāfat*.

I would also like to make it clear why this vision should not be considered to be from Satan. The reason being, in the first place, the Promised Messiah[as] himself viewed it as very significant and noted it down in his notebook. Secondly, the dream saw literal fulfilment within a period of two years. A vision that gets fulfilled in such a glorious manner cannot be from Satan. Should it be from Satan, what difference then will there be left between a satanic vision and a divine one? Moreover, what shall then prevent people from dubbing every vision as satanic?

Second Heavenly Testimony

In 1909, I was not yet fully aware of any dispute regarding *Khilāfat*. However, on the fifteenth day of the *Khilāfat* of Ḥaḍrat Khalīfatul-Masīḥ I[ra] someone raised the subject with me and said, 'We should begin to think as to what rights a *Khalīfah* should have.' I told him, 'The time to do that was when the institution of *Khilāfat* had not been established. Now, after we have taken *bai'at*, how can we, as mere servants, determine the rights of our master? How can we limit the rights of the one to whom we have pledged allegiance?' From then on no one ever took issues with me on this subject, and I completely forgot the above mentioned incident, until the time came in 1909 when I saw a vision that there was a large house wherein everything was complete and ready to be used except for the roof which still had to be finished. The concrete rods on the roof had already been placed, but what was still left to be done was to have the bricks clayed and pressed hard against each other to ensure they remained tightly fixed in their place. The rods seemed to have been covered with some straw, and Mir Muhammad Ishaq appeared to be standing just a short distance from them. I saw him accompanied by Mian Bashir Ahmad, Nisar Ahmad [late] son of Pir Iftikhar Ahmad of Ludhiana. Mir Muhammad Ishaq appeared to be carrying a packet of matchboxes in his hand and it looked as if he intended to set that straw on fire. I told him not to do that lest the rods should catch fire. I told him that the straw would surely be burnt sometime in the future, but not at this time. Having told him emphatically not to do so and being satisfied at heart that he would follow my advice, I left the place. I had not yet gone too far when I heard some noise from behind. When I turned around, I found Mir Muhammad Ishaq taking out some match sticks from the matchbox and rubbing them against the packet in order to set them alight, but failing to do so. Then he took out a few more sticks out and tried rubbing them against the packet wishing to set fire to the straw as soon as possible. I ran to him to stop him but before I got there, he had already set it ablaze. I jumped into the fire and was able to put it out, but in the meantime the tops of three rods were burnt anyway.

I related this dream of mine to Maulavī Sayyed Sarwar Shah the same afternoon. He smiled and said that the dream had already been fulfilled. Therewith, he told me that Mir Muhammad Ishaq had prepared some questions and given them to Ḥaḍrat Khalīfatul-Masīḥ[ra] for their answers, and that the questions have caused a great uproar in the Jamā'at. I then wrote what I had seen in my vision to Ḥaḍrat Khalīfatul-Masīḥ[ra]. He read it and said that it had already come true, and wrote down the incident in detail for me on a piece of paper. After I had read it, he took it back from me and tore it up. Maulavī Sayyed Sarwar Shah is the witness to this vision. Anyone can enquire from him whether these incidents had really taken place. And so it was that this vision was literally fulfilled. The answers given by Ḥaḍrat Khalīfatul-Masīḥ I[ra] exposed the hypocrisy of some people. God Almighty, in His grace, put out the dangerous fire which was about to engulf the Jamā'at. However, the tops of certain rods could not survive and were eventually burnt, and the fire of jealousy kept burning the hearts of the hypocrites. This dream also contained the news that the straw would eventually be put on fire and burnt down; and that is what happened.

Third Heavenly Testimony

There was no plan as yet of calling any public meeting to discuss this subject, although the dispute regarding *Khilāfat* had already started. Meanwhile, I saw a vision that there was a public meeting which Ḥaḍrat Khalīfatul-Masīḥ I[ra] was addressing, and that his speech was on the subject of *Khilāfat*. Some of the audience were opposed to him. I moved forward and while standing on his right submitted to him: 'Ḥuḍūr! You need not worry. We shall lay down our lives for you and none shall be able to reach you unless they have to jump over our dead bodies. We are your humblest servants.' I then related this dream of mine to Ḥaḍrat Khalīfatul-Masīḥ I[ra].

When the proposal for the public meeting came, the members of the Jamā'at started assembling in Qadian to discuss the issue of *Khilāfat*. Ḥaḍrat Khalīfatul-Masīḥ I[ra] stood up to say a few words on this occasion. I was sitting to his left. He told me to sit on his right in accordance with what I had seen in my dream. He also told me to say a few words after he finished speaking. My words were to the effect that we were his most obedient servants.

Fourth Heavenly Testimony

Much earlier than the time when the dispute regarding *Khilāfat* began I had seen the vision that I mentioned earlier and which the Promised Messiah[as] had noted down [in his note book] in his own handwriting. Also, I had seen the dream in which God Almighty gave the good news of the burning of some of the heads of the hypocrites as a consequence of the questions raised by Mir Muhammad Ishaq. Despite all this, I felt heavy at heart and wished that God may reveal to me the details of the impending confrontation. Therefore, I repeatedly prayed to God about it. I wished God may explained to me the details of the problems destined to appear in the future. I repeatedly prayed to God for the truth to be revealed to me, and reality to be manifested. I beseeched Him to reveal the truth no matter who is favoured, for I was not bound by any party, rather, I only wanted God to be pleased with me. I kept praying in this way during the days preceding the public meeting, but was not informed of anything. But then the night came and the next morning the meeting was due to begin and the questions were going to be read out. That night I became extremely restless and my heart was beating faster than usual. I became truly worried, for I did not know what to do. That night, I wept bitterly before my Lord and submitted to Him that the issue was going to be discussed in the morning, and that I wished He would guide me about the party who was in the right. I prayed that though at that time I considered *Khilāfat* to be in the right, my sole desire was to please my Lord and that I was not going to be insistent on any belief. I only wished that God Himself would reveal to me how to resolve the issue so that my heart may feel consoled. The words that flowed on my tongue in the morning, by God's decree, were:[14]

قُلْ مَا يَعْبَؤُا بِكُمْ رَبِّي لَوْلَا دُعَآؤُكُمْ ۚ

That is, 'Say [to the believers] My Lord would not care for you.' Therewith, I felt solaced and considered myself to be in the right. The word *qul* [meaning: say] in the beginning of the verse had assured me that the conclusion of mine was absolutely correct. I understood that by using the word God wanted me to inform people about the divine command that I had received. Had I been in the wrong, the words of the revelation must have been without the word, *qul* in the beginning of the verse. I had told many people about the specific words of the dream, but at the moment I cannot recall the names of all of them.

Fifth Heavenly Testimony

Furthermore, I had a vision three years prior to the demise of Ḥaḍrat Khalīfatul-Masīḥ I[ra], the interpretation of which was that his will would bear some relationship with Nawwāb Ṣāḥib. God caused that vision to be fulfilled after three years' time and proved that He is All-Powerful.

---

[14] *Sūrah al-Furqān*, 25:78

Sixth Heavenly Testimony

In September, 1913, I was in Simla for a few days. At the time of my departure from Qadian, Ḥaḍrat Khalīfatul-Masīḥ I[ra] was in good health. Then just one or two days after I had arrived in Simla, I had a vision in which I saw that I was sitting in my room [in Qadian] and the time was around 2 o'clock. I saw that Mirza Abdul-Ghafoor, who lived in Kalanour, came to see me and called my name from downstairs. I asked him about the purpose of his visit. He said that Ḥaḍrat Khalīfatul-Masīḥ[ra] was seriously ill and was running a temperature around 102 degrees. He said that he was sent by him to inform me that he had published his will in *al-Badr*, and that I could see it printed in the paper in March. I got extremely worried and for a moment thought of immediately returning to Qadian. But then I thought it would be appropriate to first confirm whether Ḥaḍrat Khalīfatul-Masīḥ[ra] was really ill. So I sent a telegram and enquired about his health. Ḥuḍūr wrote back that he was feeling well.

Later, I related this vision to Nawwāb Muhammad Ali Khan, Chief of the State of Maler Kotla, and Sayyed Sarwar Shah. I think someone from the sons of Nawwāb Muhammad Ali, such as Mian Abdur-Rahman Khan, Mian Abdullah Khan or Mian Abdur-Rahim Khan was also present on the occasion when I had related this dream. In fact, there were many people sitting around me when I related it.

One must now reflect how God Almighty informed me of Ḥaḍrat Khalīfatul-Masīḥ's[ra] demise and how He revealed to me four distinctive signs in this regard. They were such that none could ever have discovered them by way of his own imagination or conjecture.

- First, I was informed that he would die of fever.
- Second, that he would be able to write his will before his demise.
- Third, that it will be published in the month of March and,
- Fourth that it will have something to do with *al-Badr*.

I think it would not be inappropriate if, at this point, I include the fifth sign as well, i.e., that this vision was also related to me in one way or the other; for if that were not the case, what could be the purpose of sending that man to me and conveying the information to me [as seen in dream]. Moreover, it contained such a message as no one was able to understand before it actually took place. But when the actual incident took place accordingly, the dream was proven to be true. It is now very clear that this vision also contained the indication of my *Khilāfat*. No thought regarding this had ever crossed my mind, so I could not have imagined anything like this at the time that I saw the vision.

Out of the five inferences made from this vision, four are very clear. For example, his dying of fever happened accordingly. As for the will, that too is quite obvious, because he had it written down before his demise. The third sign, i.e., its publication in the month of March, too, has no ambiguity, for he wrote it in the month of March and it was published the same month. The fifth sign—its bearing some relationship with me—was also fulfilled in accordance with the vision. But the fourth distinction, i.e., the reference to *Badr* requires some elaboration, for although his will was published in *al-Fazl*, *al-Ḥakm* and *Nūr*, it was not published in *Badr*, which was not being published at that time. Hence, what shall we understand from 'Look it up in *Badr*'? One must remember that at times the dreams and visions are fulfilled literally and at times they have to be interpreted. This vision also is such that it has to be interpreted. Four of the distinctive signs mentioned in the vision had really come true, but there remains one sign that was yet to be interpreted. But the fulfilment of other four signs had already sealed the truth of the vision. As for the interpretation of the remaining one sign, let me explain that the moon on the fifteenth night of its cycle is called *Badr*. But in order to partly conceal the message in the vision, God named the fourteenth night of March as Badr according to the fourteenth night of the lunar circle. This told us that the incident would take place on the fourteenth. The date the will was formally announced was the 14th—it was on that day that the trustee of the will, Nawwāb Muhammad Ali Khan, read out the will to the public. The decision regarding the continuation of the institution of *Khilāfat* was also made on this same day.

Seventh Heavenly Testimony

About three or four years ago I had another vision wherein I saw myself aboard a car. The car was moving towards our house. Meanwhile, somebody told me of the demise of Ḥaḍrat Khalīfatul-Masīḥ I[ra]. I told the driver of the car to go faster so that I could reach home at the earliest. I had also narrated this vision to many of my friends before the demise of Ḥaḍrat Khalīfatul-Masīḥ I[ra]. I can still recall the names of some of those people. They were Nawwāb Muhammad Ali Khan, Maulavī Sayyed Sarwar Shah, Sheikh

Yaqoob Ali, Ḥāfiz Roshan Ali, and probably Master Muhammad Sharif B.A., Pleader, Chief Court, Lahore. In the meantime, I had to travel to Lahore for an important task in connection with Ḥuḍūr's illness. I thought it was improper to leave since Ḥuḍūr[ra] was not feeling well. I discussed the matter with my friends and told them that I did not want to travel since I had seen in the vision that I came to know about Ḥuḍūr's demise during my journey. I feared that the incident might take place when I was still on my way. So, I sent someone else to take care of the task. But who can prevent the will of God from happening? Since Ḥuḍūr[ra] was staying in Nawwāb Ṣāḥib's house, I too stayed with him and visited Qadian only for the Friday prayers. The day that Ḥaḍrat Khalīfatul-Masīḥ I[ra] passed away, I was in Qadian as usual to lead the Friday Prayers. As was my habit, I prepared myself to go back by the road which went through the market. Meanwhile, news came from Nawwāb Ṣāḥib that he was waiting for me in the Ahmadiyya Maḥallah and that he wanted to see me. When I got there, his car was already standing by and he sat down in it along with me and was accompanied by Dr. Khalīfah Rashīdud-Dīn, Assistant Surgeon. The car then left for his bungalow, and just as it approached the road that passes through the ground of Ta'līmul-Islam School, one of his servants rushed to us and broke the news of Ḥaḍrat Khalīfatul-Masīḥ I[ra] demise. Grief overcame me and I told the driver to speed up the car and try to reach there as soon as possible. Nawwāb Ṣāḥib suddenly recalled the dream and said that it had been fulfilled.

This vision is such an overwhelming proof of God's existence that it is a source of great wisdom and guidance for every rational person, except the one who is stone-hearted and thereby refuses to accept the truth. It also makes it clear that however one may try to avoid the destiny ordained by God, it never fails, and does take place no matter what the circumstances. The fate, fearing which I had adjourned the plan of travelling to Lahore, came to pass anyway while I was still in Qadian.

Eighth Heavenly Testimony

Three or four years later I had a vision in which I saw that Ḥāfiz Roshan Ali[ra] and I were sitting at some place, and it seemed as if the British Government had appointed me the Commander In Chief of the Army. I had been appointed after Sir Omor Kray, the Ex. Commander In Chief of the Indian Army, and the charge was being given to me by Ḥāfiz Roshan Ali[ra] on behalf [of the British government]. While taking the charge, I expressed some reservations about taking it pointing towards some flaw in it. I said that in the presence of the flaw how was it possible for me to take the charge? Just as I said these words, the floor beneath me opened (we were standing on the roof), and I saw Ḥaḍrat Khalīfatul-Masīḥ I[ra] appearing from the opening. At that moment, I considered him to be Sir Omor Kray, the Ex. Commander In Chief of the Indian Army. Referring to the flaw, he spoke to me saying, 'It is not my fault. In fact, I have inherited it from Lord Kitchner.'

I always wondered what the vision meant. I would narrate it to my friends and ask them what it could possibly mean. But such are the ways of the Almighty that I came to know about its meaning only after the actual incidents took place. I found that the incidents served as a great testimony in favour of the choice that was made by the Jamā'at after the demise of Ḥaḍrat Khalīfatul-Masīḥ I[ra] and was in accordance with the divine will. When Ḥaḍrat Khalīfatul-Masīḥ

I[ra] passed away, I felt that the vision was in fact a great prophecy, and it contained the tiding that after Ḥaḍrat Maulavī Ṣāḥib[ra], the office of *Khilāfat* will be assigned to me. This was the reason why Ḥaḍrat Khalīfatul-Masīḥ I[ra] was shown to me dressed like Sir Omor Kray. So far as the command of the army is concerned, that meant leadership of the Jamā'at, for the Jamā'ats of the Prophets too are armies through whom God causes the faith to prevail. Due to this vision, I hope that the propagation of true Islam will, God willing, take place at the hands of the Ahmadiyya Jamā'at and not at the hands of the rebels of *Khilāfat*, with the exception of only a few of those whom God may wish to grant some partial success. But there is no doubt that the blessings that will be vouchsafed to the efforts of those who will submit to *Khilāfat* will be overwhelming as compared to those who would receive them only partially.

When considered further, the vision appears to be such a great testimony from the Divine that the more one reflects upon it, the more it appears to exhibit the glory of God Almighty. The reason is that the Promised Messiah[as] has been shown as Lord Kitchner in this vision, and Ḥaḍrat Khalīfatul-Masīḥ I[ra] as Sir Omar Kray. When we look at the career of these two people, we find that Lord Kitchner left India the same year the Promised Messiah[as] had passed away, and Sir Omar Kray was appointed as Commander in Chief in his place. This was but one aspect of the interpretation. What is even more surprising is the fact that the year and the month in which Sir Omar Kray left India was March 1914. It was the same month and year in which Ḥaḍrat Khalīfatul-Masīḥ I[ra] passed away and God had appointed me his successor. Can anyone possessed of virtue and piety say that the vision was a satanic one; or can anyone imagine a human being able to fabricate such a vision some two or three years prior to the occurrence of the incident? Could it ever be possible? Was it possible for me to fabricate all these incidents and relate them to people two years prior to their occurrence? Moreover, how was it possible for those same incidents to have then come true? Who could have informed me that Ḥaḍrat Maulavī Ṣāḥib[ra] would depart from this world in the month of March, and that the incident would take place in the year 1914, and that I would become his successor? Is there anyone who could make all this possible except the Almighty God? None, at all!

The flaw which the vision showed in the charge and my aversion to accepting it was indicative of the small number of people who were to create the disorder. God Almighty, through this vision, cleared Ḥaḍrat Maulavī Ṣāḥib[ra] of the objection made against him by such elements. These critics believe the present-day disorder would not have taken place if, in stead of making mere hints at the inner condition of these people, Ḥaḍrat Khalīfatul-Masīḥ I[ra] had openly informed them of their hypocrisy or if he had expelled them from the Jamā'at. God Almighty himself spoke on his behalf and informed me that the fault had not emerged during his time; rather, he had inherited it [when he became *Khalīfah*]. So, in my dream he had to convey to me that the people concerned had gone astray during the life time of the Promised Messiah[as], and that he was not responsible for their misconduct in any way.

Here, someone may raise the objection that the interpretation is being made contemporaneously. It must be remembered that the interpretation comes to be known only after an incident has actually taken place. In case of this particular vision, it is indeed very clear, and there is no ambiguity. Everyone will agree that there can be no valid interpretation except the one which I have put forward.

I had related this vision to Ḥāfiz Roshan Ali[ra] ahead of time. There were some other friends also whom I had told about it, but I have forgotten their names.

Ninth Heavenly Testimony

Just as God had informed me before time of the dispute regarding *Khilāfat*, the demise of Ḥaḍrat Khalīfatul-Masīḥ I[ra], his will and my succession, He also informed me regarding those who were to rebel against me and create turmoil. I was also informed that these people were doomed to fail in their efforts. This happened about seven years ago.

It was in the month of October or November of 1902 during the lifetime of the Promised Messiah[as]. I saw that I was either in a room of the boarding house or in the office of *The Review of Religions*. There I saw Maulavī Muhammad Ali sitting on a large suit case and found myself standing at some distance from him. Meanwhile, I saw Sheikh Rahmatullah coming through the door. Having found us together he asked if I was taller or Maulavī Muhammad Ali. Maulavī Ṣāḥib replied that he was taller than me. Hearing this, I claimed that I was taller. Sheikh Rahmatullah said, 'Let us measure you both.' I saw that Maulavī Ṣāḥib wanted to come down from the suite case, but like children who find it hard to get down from an elevated bed, Maulavī Ṣāḥib descended with some difficulty. When Sheikh Rahmatullah lined us both together, he amazedly said, 'I thought Maulavī Ṣāḥib was taller, but I have found you to be taller than him.' I reiterated that I was certainly taller than him. Later, he said that he wanted to lift Maulavī Ṣāḥib and take him up to my shoulders to see how far his feet reached. So he lifted him up in order to bring him parallel to my shoulders, but the more he lifted him up, the more I grew in height. Eventually, with great effort, he managed to bring him up to my shoulders, but then saw that Maulavī Ṣāḥib's legs barely reached my knees. This surprised Sheikh Rahmatullah a great deal.

I had this vision at a time when disputes could not have even been imagined. It is not for a man to tell what will happen after seven years. I had related this vision to Sayyed Sarwar Shah[ra], Sayyed Wali'ullah Shah[ra] who is currently in Beirut, Syria, and Sayyed Habibullah Shah who is studying in the final year of Medical College. They can be asked to give their testimony in this regard. Hopefully, they will still be able recall the vision. I had possibly narrated it to some other friends as well, but for the time being I am not so sure of their names. We used to wonder what this measuring of heights meant. There was neither any question of *Khilāfat* nor of taking allegiance to any *Khalīfah*. The Promised Messiah[as] was still alive. Who could imagine that the circumstances would change so dramatically and that an entirely different situation would emerge? But, the Words of God are always fulfilled. Maulavī Muhammad Ali's friends encouraged him to stand against me, but God Almighty caused all of their work to come to naught. Consequently, they themselves confessed to their being abased and frustrated. The more his friends tried to raise his morale, the more God caused him to suffer. God also made about ninety-seven percent of Aḥmadīs submit to my *Khilāfat*, and created unity among the members of the Jamā'at through me, thereby causing me to emerge far more superior to Maulavī Muhammad Ali.

Now, in the end, I suggest to all the truth-loving people that if they have not been able to reach any decision regarding *Khilāfat* until now, they should make the decision now. For it is God who has appointed the *Khalīfah* and no man has anything to do with it. If you deny this truth, then you will have to deny the truth of the Promised Messiah[as]. Therefore, accept the truth and do not cause discord amongst the Jamā'at. I am but a humble servant of the Jamā'at through whom God wills to bring unity to its members. Otherwise, as for this work, that is all of God. I never wanted to be a *Khalīfah*, nor do I have any obsession about it now. God Himself appointed me to perform this task. It is not due to my own efforts that I have attained this position. Therefore, you must understand that while God had already informed me of the dispute regarding *Khilāfat*, the Divine support for it, the year and the month of the demise of Ḥaḍrat Khalīfatul-Masīḥ I[ra], his will, my hearing of his death in the car as well as the condition of his illness; how on earth was it possible for me to have any doubt about divine plans even for a second? This was besides the fact that certain other visions had already been fulfilled making it clear to me that the divine Will wanted me to be the next *Khalīfah* [after Ḥaḍrat Khalīfatul-Masīḥ I[ra]]. While the vision had clearly foretold that I would be opposed, yet succeed, how could I then pay any attention to the words of those people who advised me to abandon the robe of *Khilāfat*? Can I act against the Will of God? As a matter of fact, if I do so, I will be rejecting God's decision in this regard. May Allah guard me against any such move. What God willed, came to pass; and what people desired, did not come to pass. Blessed indeed is he who accepts the verdict of God and does not try to stubbornly reject the testimonies that have come from God.

(The Remaining part of the First Speech Delivered after the Ẓuhr and ʿAṣr Prayers on December 27, 1914)

Important Issues Facing the Jamāʿat

After reciting *tashahhud, taʿawwudh*, and *Sūrah al-Fātiḥah*, Ḥuḍūr[ra] said:

How Gracious is our Lord towards Muslims and how magnanimously He treats His servants that a true Muslim can never suffer humiliation against anyone in any matter. Unwarranted prejudice, stubbornness and rigidity are utterly despicable and contemptible, but God has bestowed Muslims with such high spiritual stations that no one belonging to another faith can ever attain the loftiness of spirituality equal to them. I was going to speak on some other subject, but happened to recall something while reciting *Sūrah al-Fātiḥah* which I am now going to relate.

Human beings, on account of their limited knowledge, commit many errors in making their decisions. There was a time when people believed that the heavens were made of different metals. Later, philosophers suggested that the heavens only marked the endpoint to which a human eye could see, and that there was nothing physical about them. They said that no one knew what else could be discovered in the days to come. That is how all fields of knowledge are shaped. The branches of knowledge that existed a hundred years ago do not exist any more; instead, some new fields have emerged with the passage of time. Initially, it was believed that the universe consisted of just one sun, and that all other stars and planets revolved around the same sun; but now we have come to know that there are stars which are so huge and so far away from us that their light is just reaching us now. Moreover, they are much bigger in size than the sun. At one time, people used to believe, and it is a well-known premise, that the pointer of a compass always faced north; but now experiments have revealed that at certain intervening periods it starts moving towards the west as well, and having travelled in that direction for some time it again changes its course and turns towards the north. In short, knowledge is undergoing such rapid changes that what we know today may prove to be wrong tomorrow. There is no doubt that God has blessed man with knowledge and wisdom, but He has certainly not endowed an intellect which is infallible and which cannot accept changes to the conclusions it has drawn already. This is why God has taught Muslims how to pray, because humans being are prone to making mistakes. Instead of praying to God that something must be given to them or some work must be done for them; God has taught that they should pray that God may cause to happen that which is good in His estimation, and that may He provide them with that which is truly beneficial. Since God never makes mistakes, His decision is always right and correct. To turn towards God is the simplest and best method available to everyone in this world to make the best decisions in regard to every matter. To us, also, this is the simplest method available. Anyone who had failed to understand the philosophy of *Khilāfat* should have prayed to God, and performed *Istikhārah*, beseeching God for guidance and submitting to Him, 'O my Lord! If the right path is that of *Khilāfat*, pray do let me know. If not, show me the straight path, and do not let me off the path of the righteous lest I go astray.' But, alas! There are many who did not give heed to this method. I told many of my friends about this method and they acted upon it and received guidance from Allah through some dream or revelation, or God blessed their hearts with satisfaction and conviction in some other way. If someone is still in doubt and feels apprehensive, he can still follow this same method. God will surely guide him on the right path.

In my first speech, I was only able to highlight one point, but there are fourteen more points to speak on. Four of them require the same time to explain as the first one, but I have neither the strength nor the time needed to do so. In addition, there is another important point to be discussed tomorrow. By the grace of Allah, I am feeling relieved of the cough, but I have started feeling some pain in the chest. Therefore, I would like to explain the remaining points more concisely. God willing, I shall speak on them in greater detail at some other time.

Politics

One more thing that I must speak on is politics. There is a great confusion in our Jamā'at over this issue, and lack of clear guidance has been a great trial for some. Questions as to whether or not we should take part in politics, and whether politics is good; or if it is bad, just how bad it is; all these questions have been a source of much controversy. In light of this growing confusion, I reflected upon the teachings of the Promised Messiah[as], and asked his companions for their opinion on the matter. They are unable to quote even a single example whereby the Promised Messiah[as] ever instructed them to focus their attention on politics, or told them to pursue it. However, it raises another objection, and this objection is not only repeated by the newly educated youth, but by some experienced people also. The objection is: why is the Ahmadiyya Jamā'at not allowed to take part in politics?

Why is the Ahmadiyya Jamā'at Not Allowed to Take Part in Politics?

An ignorant and unwise person may say that Aḥmadīs are told not to take part in it because it is a useless waste of time, but a person who has studied history and who is well-informed regarding the peoples of the past will never make such a comment, for he knows that worldly governments and rulers depend upon politics. God Almighty has also stated some benefits of politics in the Holy Quran. The Holy Quran has considered this topic worthy of discussion for it found it to be something beneficial; else, why would it have mentioned it? Moreover, we also observe that strikes often help people secure their rights. Governments, too, do not mind agitation as long as it is justifiable. The question then is, why is the Jamā'at not allowed to take part in politics, and why has the Promised Messiah[as] forbidden us to pursue it?

First of all, I do not consider politics to be useless outright. However, the difference between my opinion and that of others is that I do not see the same benefits that others do. Since I am afraid this controversy could result in discord amongst the members of the Jamā'at, I wish to explain the reality of this particular point of view so that, God willing, the matter can be resolved once and for all.

The Holy Quran sets out an easy way to decide on any matter, which is, that before making any decision, one should seriously consider all the advantages and disadvantages that may ensue. The Holy Quran, in relation to gambling and drinking, states:[1]

يَسْـَٔلُوْنَكَ عَنِ الْخَمْرِ وَالْمَيْسِرِ ؕ قُلْ فِيْهِمَآ اِثْمٌ كَبِيْرٌ وَّمَنَافِعُ لِلنَّاسِ ۫
وَ اِثْمُهُمَآ اَكْبَرُ مِنْ نَّفْعِهِمَا …

That is, people ask you about drinking and whether it is lawful to drink or forbidden, and similarly they ask you about gambling. God instructed His Prophet[sa] to tell them that both carry some good qualities as well as some bad qualities. But the disadvantages outweigh the advantages. How pure is the religion of Islam! It never closes its eyes from even the slightest good and virtuous qualities that a thing may have. How beautifully and truly it has answered the question. Upon the question being asked, it has not forbidden drinking and gambling outright, but it has made clear that the drawbacks far outnumber the benefits. Then it has left the decision up to you. The formula that God has laid down for us is that everything is possessed of two kinds of attributes, those that are

---

1 They ask thee concerning wine and the game of hazard. Say: 'In both there is great sin and also *some* advantages for men; but their sin is greater than their advantage.' (*Sūrah al-Baqarah*, 2:220)

beneficial as well as those that detrimental. For this reason, it instructs us to do something only when the advantages exceed the disadvantages. It also advises us to shun those things whose negative aspects are more than the positive ones. All of the world's enterprises move according to this doctrine. Every single person opts for that which carries greater benefit and avoids that which is likely to cause risk or damage. Therefore, you should judge politics on the same principle. Politics, in itself, is not a bad thing at all. But, our point of view is that a thing lawful at one time can become unlawful at another. For instance, through prayer one attains nearness to God, but sometimes the same person becomes Satan by offering the same prayer at sunrise or sunset. In such a situation, he becomes Satan rather than attaining nearness to God. God says that He Himself becomes the reward for a person who fasts for His sake, but the Holy Prophet[sa] has said that those who fast on the Eid day are Satans. So, although fasting for the sake of God is indeed a great form of worship, to fast on the Eid day has been declared a satanic act by the Holy Prophet[sa]. It is obvious that a thing which is good at one time can become bad at another. For instance, if someone suffering from backache requests someone else to massage his back to relieve the pain and thereby receive a reward in return, the massager will surely get a reward; but if someone is busy speaking to some gathering and his servant while sitting to his back starts massaging him, then could you anticipate the treatment the servant will get from his master? The servant will be punished, because everything is meant to be done at its appropriate time.

In other words, something which is considered to be bad at one time can become good at another. The reason why the Promised Messiah[as] forbade his Jamā'at from taking part in politics was that the time was not yet ripe for such an activity. Therefore, despite the fact that the government encourages participation in politics, it is still improper for us to engage in it. The Promised Messiah[as] wrote that though the government permits indulging in political matters to some extent, he saw that the end of such indulgence was going to be harmful. That is why I too do not permit my Jamā'at to take part in it. Once the Promised Messiah[as] went to see a high official of the province. Although it was not his practice to go and see such people, he went this time considering the official to be his guest. The government in those days considered the Muslim League to be of some benefit to the state in the future. The official asked the Promised Messiah[as] of his opinion about the Muslim League. He answered that he did not know about it. Khawaja Ṣāḥib had recently acquired its membership so he drew a very rosy picture of it before the Promised Messiah[as]. The Promised Messiah[as] remarked that he did not really like that people take part in politics. The official said, 'the Muslim League is nothing bad. It bodes well'. The Promised Messiah[as] replied: 'How do you say it is not bad? A day will come when it will also stand against you.' The official said, 'Maybe you have Congress in your mind. The League is not like Congress; for the result of anything depends upon the principles it is founded on. Congress proved to be harmful since its foundation rested on wrong principles, but the Muslim League stands on doctrines which shall never allow any kind of rebellious element to take root in it.' The Promised Messiah[as] replied that this might be what he thought today, but the League would soon behave in the same way as Congress.

Now, certain incidents have proved that the Muslim League is also inclining towards demanding self-rule which the Congress had been seeking for a long time. However, it is possible that the Muslim League may be using some other term for it. In short, even though an official who held a responsible position greatly emphasized that the Muslim League would not be harmful, the Promised Messiah[as] reiterated that their activities would not result in something good. Eventually, his statement proved to be true. Remember it well that the reason why the Promised Messiah[as] has stopped his Jamā'at from taking an even legitimate interest in politics is not that politics is bad in itself; rather, he did it keeping in view its being more harmful than beneficial at this particular juncture. Here, I will continue to explain this point even further.

There is a *hadith* which says:

ستكون اثرة وامور تنكرونها قالوا يارسول اللّٰه فما تأمرنا
قال تؤدون الحق الذى عليكم وتسألون اللّٰه الذى لكم

That is, a time will come when such rulers will appear who will desire everything good only for themselves and will pay no attention to the comfort of the ordinary people, and such things will appear which you will abhor. The companions of the Holy Prophet[sa] submitted, 'O Prophet of God! What are we supposed to do in such a situation?' That is, they asked whether they should stand against such rulers and forcefully put them on the right track. The Holy Prophet[sa] said, 'Do fulfil your obligations which you owe to the rulers, and as for the rights which they owe to you, do not demand it of them. Let God Himself take care of your needs, and pray that may He be your help.'

On the other hand, there is another *hadith* also which says:

من قتل دون عرضه وماله فهو شهيد

The one who dies protecting his honour and wealth is a martyr.

So on the one hand, he who dies protecting his wealth and honour is called a martyr, and on the other hand people are being asked to stay patient in the face of cruelties committed by their rulers and not to stand against them despite their atrocities. The Holy Prophet[sa] is commanding the people not to beg for even their legitimate rights; rather, he advises them to leave everything to God. Studying these traditions side by side, one realizes that these two commandments are meant to be followed at different occasions. At one time, people have been commanded to forcefully seek their rights, and at another, they have been advised to silently accept whatever is given to them. Let alone engaging in a fight with the rulers, people have been told to not even demand for any basic rights. The reason for this is that sometimes governments undergo a period of trouble, and their condition becomes so fragile that they can save themselves only if they revert to their previous state of affairs; otherwise were they to bring about some change—even if it is a noteworthy one or leads to betterment—it ultimately proves to be disastrous, because it exposes the weakness of that system of government. In such a situation, uprisings in the country would definitely result in the collapse of the government. Therefore, in such a situation, the Holy Prophet[sa] has forbidden Muslims to demand even their most basic rights from their rulers, lest the demands result in the very destruction of the government. But at times when the situation is different, he allows the demanding of rights under certain conditions. Similarly, the commandments of the Promised Messiah[as] need to be followed in accordance with the prevailing conditions.

What is Politics

A storyteller writes that once there was a wall. Anyone who climbed it and looked down the other side of it never returned, for he convulsed with laugher and tumbled down. Of course, there is no truth to the story of there actually being such a wall. But should we reflect further upon this story, we find that there is such a wall, and that wall is politics. Man is impetuous by nature and tends to adore what reaps quick benefits for him and does not like those things for which he has to wait. That is why people indulge in activities which bring about quick gains. So when someone sees that politics speeds up material gains such as wealth, political authority and status, they begin to chase after it blindly. The case is similar to that of a lion. They say about lion that once it has tasted the blood of a human, it keeps on hunting for humans again and again. Initially, the sight of but one or two persons would make it flee, but later it does not care even if there are thirty or forty people. Similarly, one who has tasted of the blood of politics finds it hard to break himself away from it, and continues pursuing it ceaselessly.

Politics Causes One to Neglect Other Things

On the one hand, politics causes one to neglect every other thing, even one's own life. It keeps drawing one to itself. On the other hand, Islam has never been as vulnerable at any time in the past as it is today. Therefore, today, Islam is in need of as many people as possible to help it and as many warriors as possible to protect it, for it can never have enough. The indulgence of Muslims in politics at this point of time is such a poison, the consuming of which will make it hard, nay impossible, for them to survive. Politics demands too much attention, and those who indulge in it get absolutely lost in it. The war going on in Europe today is such that every country is trying to provide as many soldiers to fight as it can, even women and young boys and girls are being trained to provide assistance. A small number of soldiers are not going to be enough for such a terrible and dangerous war. But, the war which is faced by Islam today is much larger in scale than that of Europe. Islam is alone in its fight against the whole world, and the enemy is so strong that it can bring thousands of soldiers to battle against a single soldier of Islam. Even the Muslims are getting estranged from Islam and are Muslims only in name. They are as far from Islam as the people of other religions are from their own faiths. Hence, a mere few are not going to achieve any success in this war; rather, every old one and young one and every woman should get ready to take part in it. When a house is on fire, it is not the water bearer who is called to extinguish the fire just because it is his job to provide water and is paid for doing so. Rather, at that time, everyone runs towards water to collect it so as to spray it on the fire and extinguish it, and even women and children get involved to help. Similarly, today the enemy has set fire to the house of Islam. He is certainly foolish who waits for mere water bearers to come and extinguish it. This enormous fire that has engulfed the house of Islam from every angle cannot be extinguished by a handful of people. Rather, every person with even an iota of faith in his heart is under the obligation to work on extinguishing this fire. It is the obligation of every one of you, whether you are a man or woman, old or young, boy or girl, to stand up and put out this fire. Those who are guilty of being remiss at this juncture are certainly not of Islam. Had the Promised Messiah[as] allowed people to take part in political affairs at a time when Islam had become so vulnerable, a large portion of the Jamā'at might have gotten involved in it and held back from serving Islam; whereas Islam is in dire need of their help, and the number of its army is already small, how can it spare even a portion of it for another task? Foolish is he, who having viewed both the struggle that is going on in politics and the condition that Islam is suffering in, still indulges in politics. When will he find time to serve religion? Since people earn high standing and fame quickly in politics, they shun even their faith for the sake of the benefit at hand. In addition, the world is ever more attractive in this age. However much one gets drawn towards politics, it is never considered enough. It is for this reason that the Promised Messiah[as] did not allow himself to let go of even those few who were with him by permitting them to join politics. Should someone say that abandoning politics may cause him to suffer losses, in that he will not be able to become a Tehsildar or Deputy Commissioner or attain another official post, he should remember that abandoning these things will lead him to God; whereas clinging to them will bring him the world. Therefore, shun politics if God is dearer to you; but if you wish to attain the pleasures at hand which are of this world, then do what you consider is best for you. We have no right to forcefully stop you from taking part in it.

Politics Involves Grouping and Lobbying

Politics involves grouping and lobbying. If a group of people stand together and ask the government to fulfil their demands and put forth their agenda in clear terms, only then are their demands heard. However, in every matter, the government considers which point of view is being supported by the majority of the people. Therefore, if the people make demands today, the government will only listen and fulfil the demands of those who can prove that they are in majority. But as for you, consider your circumstances. What strength do you have, compared to others, to force the government to give you your rights? At present, our condition is such that when some enemy mistreats us, or causes some suffering or pain to us, it is the police that come to our rescue. Remember that politics brings success only to those who enjoy a considerable majority. Should the number of students who go on strike in a school be less than those who do not follow suit, the strike will never be successful; for in that situation those who went on strike will be expelled by the administration. But there can be some hope of success if the majority of the students go on strike and then remain steadfast. Otherwise, they will meet a terrible failure. But I ask which group or party do you think is with you to help you with your cause?

Involvement in Politics Absorbs the Smaller Community into Larger Community

Experience shows that small parties joining politics have to indulge in lobbying for themselves, and as I have explained before no party can achieve success in the realm of politics unless they try to extend their lobby. This is why the small parties then mix with larger ones, but because of being small in number they get so fully absorbed in the larger parties and end up totally losing their own identity. Just take a look and you will see that all the damage that our Jamā'at has suffered is due to this very politics. Initially, a few of us joined it, but since it required so much lobbying and grouping, they had to join hands with other parties. Initially, their stance was that they would attract others to themselves, but on the contrary, they slowly began to get absorbed themselves. To begin with, they became members of the Anjuman Himayat-e-Islam, and then, when their zest for politics increased, they joined the Muslim League. Later, when they found that it would not be possible for them to gain any more success on account of our religious differences, they sacrificed their own religious beliefs in order to please the larger party and to acquire fame. Do you have any idea why they had to do this? It was nothing but the desire to gain a share in the larger lobby, the consequence of which was that for giving away their faith, they lost the world as well.

Take for example the Āryas if you want to understand this phenomenon of grouping and lobbying. In the beginning this sect interfered only in religious matters, but when the light of the modern thought guided them to the evergreen pastures of politics, they turned to it and now consider religion to be a part of politics. So much so. that today the debate is whether the Āryah religion is a religion or just a political party? Their current situation shows that they are nothing more than a political party to which religion is of no concern. They seem to have lost all their peculiarities. There was a time when they would get annoyed at those calling them Hindus. They would firmly declare themselves to be Āryas, not Hindus.

They hated being called Hindus. But having gotten involved in politics, they happily declare themselves to be Hindus just to ingratiate themselves with their Hindu brothers—those same brothers who were rather orthodox in their manners—just to be successful in politics and increase their lobby. When asked whether they are Hindus or Āryas, they harshly answer, 'what do you mean by Āryas or Hindus? We are all Hindus.' As a matter of fact, they are now joining hands with those whom they earlier used to despise and are welcoming them with open arms to extend and establish their own lobby. But this mixing up with others in order to strengthen their own group has consequently produced the same result that had been prophesied by the Promised Messiah[as], which was that day by day they will be erased, and all traces of them will be lost and the day will come when the Āryah religion will be totally gone because this nation enveloped itself in politics and politics has no religion; and so their politics will remain but their religion will disappear. In short, politics cannot function without the forming of lobbies and groups. But when a group tries to strengthen itself by including others in it, it will have to sacrifice its own distinct characteristics and when a nation loses its distinction, it loses all its glory and gets totally destroyed.

In 1907, when there were signs of a violent disturbance in the Punjab, and some mischievous people had spread fury among the public against the government, some distinguished lawyers held banquets in the honour of the Muslims sitting together with each other, eating at one place and putting aside every difference of caste or religion. Why did this take place? It only happened to extend the lobby. For those who are more deeply involved in politics, if you are to ask them what religion they follow, their answer would be that first they are Indians, then Hindus or Muslims. But can Islam ever permit Muslim to have such a stance? Definitely not! What Islam teaches us is that first and foremost we are Muslims, and then whatever else; rather, we can go further and say, we are nothing but Muslims.

Here someone may observe that there are people who take part in politics and yet manage to join religious activities; and in fact, they spend much of their time in serving their religion. Such people infer that that despite being involved in politics one can still serve his religion. As mentioned previously, one may be able to retain his relationship with religion along with being involved in politics, but politics demands lobbying and grouping, and those who are involved in it try to use religion for attaining people's sympathy. This deadens the true purpose of religion, and instead of augmenting one's faith, it causes serious damage to one's faith. Moreover, some people change their beliefs to win the pleasure of the party that enjoys the large majority. This makes them enemies of religion under the guise of friendship. Poor people, having been deceived by their proclamations, begin to see their filthy and absurd beliefs as the real and correct beliefs. Thus, the true spirit of faith is absolutely destroyed. Even if there are a few of those who tend to pay some heed to religion along with politics, they are extremely dangerous for the faith because the truth has largely diminished from the society.

Importance of Gratitude to the British Government

Then we say gratitude is something not to be forgotten in this world. The Promised Messiah[as] wrote, 'We forgot the hardship and antagonism that we had suffered under the Sikh rule when we came under the aegis of the British government.'

He also asks, who were our saviours when we were being cruelly treated by the Sikhs. Was it the Turks who came to our help? No! They were the English. At the time of the Sikh rule, people kept their religion secret and yet they were scared. But, today we declare our faith openly. One need not go into detail regarding the religious persecutions that were in existence before; let alone offering prayers in mosques, one could not even say God's name in his own house. But the British government has given us such freedom that Muslim employees are allowed to build mosques within the bona fide premises of their offices and railway stations. It is sad though that the Muslims have let this reward go to waste due to their own foolishness. Having raised the ill-timed question of permanent allotment of the given land to mosques, they have forced the government to deprive them of this freedom in the future, thereby keeping the premises of its bona fide offices and railway stations from becoming havens for religious conflicts. Such facilities would have increased in the future if the Muslims had not raised unnecessary hue and cry, and the day was not far when the Muslim employees in every office could have attained the great reward of offering prayers in congregation. In short, the British government has done us so many favours. We are leading a peaceful and comfortable life, freely discharging our religious obligations. Our biggest responsibility is to propagate our faith, and for that we have been granted every freedom. We can propagate in whatever part of the country we want. Should we ever need to travel to other countries for this purpose, the British government extends its help to us in those countries as well. Should we have to accept, though I personally do not agree with it, that the government is not willing to grant all our rights, even then one has to understand that smaller benefits are to be sacrificed for bigger benefits. There was no harm if to our estimation the Government had failed to provide us with some of our rights since we know that through this government we have been able to achieve many important rights of ours and comforts. The Muslims were being persecuted in most parts of India before the arrival of the British, and they brought them out of that condition of lowliness. Now, having attained some benefit from the British government, the Muslims should remember that they had previously lost everything, and it was the English that restored to them their lost dignity. If someone helps someone find his money, the owner of the money gives away some of it to the one who helped him locate it. The Muslims too had lost their freedom, and it was restored to them by the British. Now if they have held back certain prerogatives for themselves only, or have specified certain posts as for the English only, it is not at all appropriate to respond to the kindness and favour they have shown thus far with unreasonable commotion. Rather, civility demands that we should keep in mind their favours to us and extend our help to them. Muslims must observe patience even if the English have not bestowed upon them every right, and should be thankful to God that by His grace they have been able to secure much of what they had earlier lost through the help of the British. They had lost both their religion as well as their worldly comforts, not to mention their freedom of religion and thought. The English have given them the liberation of every kind as far as religion is concerned, whereas in worldly affairs too, they have granted them much freedom. Hence, they should have been thankful to them, and not been critical of them. For those who know the importance of religion, there is no reason to complain were the British to deny them minor jobs such as cleaning or sweeping for the Indians; for a benefactor deserves nothing but gratitude, no matter what the circumstances are, and the British have proved to be our benefactors.

Some people say that the government is obliged to give us freedom and peace to the extent that we have it today, and to do so would be for its own benefit. Therefore, the government is not doing them any favour. Our point of view is that such a stance is tantamount to saying that our parents have never done us any favour, for they had established relations with each other only to fulfil their own desire, ultimately resulting in our creation. Is it fair to say so? Of course not, never. Similarly, though we cannot deny the fact that our living peacefully is advantageous to the government, but at the same time, we cannot deny the favours it renders to us. Since it was through this government that we have been able to achieve peace and comfort we are indebted to it, and we cannot deny this fact no matter what.

Need to Stay Away from Worldly Agitation

Hence, you must remember that the Ahmadiyya Movement is not going to prosper by getting involved in or inclining to politics. Any of us who join hands with others and take part in politics will never see success, for the one who abandons God to seek after the world does not even achieve the world. Therefore, if you want to tread upon the ways of seeking nearness to God, you will never find it by seeking after the world; rather, you shall find it only by seeking after Him. God has opened the doors of His grace to us, and has raised among us the one upon whom the Holy Prophet[sa] sent his Salām [Greetings of Peace]; the one for whom many a great and righteous saints who have already departed from this world had been waiting for. God enabled us to accept him. Not only did He enable us to believe in him, but He also granted us the faculties to serve his dispensation. Hence, you are all the viceroys and lieutenant governors to the doorsteps of the Divine. You do not need any worldly titles. One who is a servant of the Promised Messiah[as] is in fact a servant of the Holy Prophet[sa], and one who is a servant of the Holy Prophet[sa] is in fact a servant of God Almighty. Your names have been counted as among those who serve God. What other matter of pride is to be attained by a person greater than this? The Holy Prophet[sa] told one of his companions that God had instructed him to teach that companion of his *Sūrah al-Fātiḥah*. The companion asked, 'O Prophet of God! Did God specifically mention my name while speaking to you?' The Holy Prophet[sa] said, 'Yes, God specifically mentioned your name.' As soon as he heard this, he started to weep profusely. He could not believe that God had considered him worthy of mention. How Benevolent is our God towards us and how Bounteous is He that He has remembered us! One, who is called upon in this world by an officer of even a low rank, finds it hard to contain his joy. But alas! The one who is called upon by God does not honour His call. God has called upon you. The worldly sovereigns and persons of rank will never be capable of giving you that which God can bestow upon you. So you should move swiftly, and being thankful to Him run towards Him when He calls upon you. Other people in this world are much better placed than you in terms of worldly wealth and luxuries, but the treasures of faith lie only with you. Others do not have them. What else do you wish to attain when you have been blessed by God to be His servants? You should be steadfast with this service and leave the worldly agitations to those who fall upon the world like insects. It is better that you engage yourselves in agitation against the Satan.

Need for Focussing on Islam and its Service

Once I travelled to Lahore to attend a marriage ceremony. Among the guests was the editor of a famous newspaper of Lahore. There was a conflict between Turkey and Austria at that time and the newspapers were arguing that the Austrian products should be boycotted. Just a few days before this marriage, I had written an essay in response to an absurd article of the same editor, whereby I had severely criticized him. When we met, he asked me how old I was. I said that I was nineteen. He was amazed to hear this and asked whether this was truly my age. This was probably due to his remembering that essay of mine. Thereafter, he asked me what our response should be about Austria which has occupied two Turkish provinces. I said that we have already been assigned a huge task [by God]. How can we divert our attention to anything else? He said that we should boycott the Austrian products, and must not buy any of the items manufactured there. It so happened that the cap which I was wearing at that time was of an Italian make. The editor said that we must not wear caps made by Austria. I told him I was not in agreement with him on this issue. Moreover, the cap I was wearing was made in Italy, and not Austria. At the time, I used to wear such caps, but the Promised Messiah[as] did not like these caps. I clearly remember that once when I wore a cap of this type on the Eid day, he looked at me and said, 'You are wearing this cap even on

Eid day!' I rushed to take it off and put on a turban. Shortly thereafter, I stopped wearing caps altogether. Anyway, the Editor insisted on boycotting the products made in countries opposed to Turkey. I said that we should first do full justice to the one boycott that we are doing at the moment, and only then we will pay attention to another. He asked me who we were boycotting. I said that we are boycotting Satan, and that in every nation Satan has taken control and is suppressing our rights with greater force every day. I said: 'Don't you ever think of boycotting him? We should first succeed in boycotting him, and then turn our attention elsewhere.' I said, 'Islam is undergoing many hardships these days, and Satan is bent upon weakening it; why are you not worried about that? Instead, you are busy boycotting Austrian goods.' Having heard this, he became silent and felt deeply ashamed.

Therefore, I would say that those who find peace in politics should go ahead with boycotting different countries; but those who love Islam cannot be concerned with anything other than severing their ties with Satan. If Islam's prosperity demanded from us the sacrifice of our wives, children, friends and acquaintances, wealth and luxury and everything else, we should readily make that sacrifice and our hearts would thereby find true solace. The Ahmadiyya community is no more than a pinch of salt as compared to the needs of Islam, nay, not even that. Therefore, if we, who are already small in number, got involved in politics, then who else would serve Islam? Let these people who indulge in politics go their way. You should involve yourselves in the service of Islam.

Recipe for Success

In the Holy Quran, God has given us the following prescription for success:[2]

وَلَقَدْ اٰتَيْنٰكَ سَبْعًا مِّنَ الْمَثَانِيْ وَالْقُرْاٰنَ الْعَظِيْمَ ○ لَا تَمُدَّنَّ عَيْنَيْكَ
اِلٰى مَا مَتَّعْنَا بِهٖٓ اَزْوَاجًا مِّنْهُمْ وَلَا تَحْزَنْ عَلَيْهِمْ وَاخْفِضْ جَنَاحَكَ
لِلْمُؤْمِنِيْنَ ○

The translation of the verse, in keeping with the spiritual station of the Holy Prophet[sa] would be that God, addressing the Holy Prophet[sa], says that: 'Since bounty has been vouchsafed to you, because you are not miserly about it—rather you are extremely generous—and in your heart you wish that it be granted to other people as well. Alas, foolish people confine themselves to their houses and do not strive to find it. You regret their condition and look towards them longingly wondering why they do not partake in the blessings of this *Sūrah*. You should instead make sure that you do not even take a glimpse at them, so that you can fully involve yourself in the training of the righteous Jamā'at that We have already given you. We shall take care of them Ourselves.'

---

2 And We have, indeed, given thee the seven oft-repeated *verses*, and the Great Quran. Stretch not thy eyes towards what We have bestowed on some classes of them to enjoy for a short time, and grieve not over them; and lower thy wing *of mercy* for the believers. (*Sūrah al-Ḥijr*, 15:88-89)

It is for this reason that God has spoken at another place as such:[3]

لَعَلَّكَ بَاخِعٌ نَّفْسَكَ اَلَّا يَكُوْنُوْا مُؤْمِنِيْنَ۝

That is: Will you grieve yourself to death because they believe not. The Holy Prophet[sa] had been vouchsafed the greatest bounty, and his greatest wish was that this bounty be spread across the whole world for everyone to accept it. That is why, at this point, God is informing him that he need not to worry if people have gone astray. God is telling him to let the believers partake of what he has. A time will come for these disbelievers when they would reap the fruit of their present actions. This is what the verse meant in keeping with the spiritual station of the Holy Prophet[sa].

In relation to us, however, the verse would mean: 'O Muslims! We have bestowed upon you great rewards and bounties. If you see someone with worldly wealth, do not become jealous and wish to acquire it for yourself. You must not look at such people with gaping eyes. What God has vouchsafed upon you is a much greater reward. Consider your condition to be the grace of God, and do not look towards whatever the materialistic people have been given. You should just leave the world for those who wish to seek it. You must not go anywhere else, since God has called you to His own threshold. Yes, you should make a living but only that which is adequate for your subsistence, for this is the command of God. Spend as much of your time in serving the faith as possible, and keep away from people whose company results in losing your

---

[3] *Sūrah ash-Shu'arā'*, 26:4

identity. You should not get involved in activities which force you to compromise your fundamental beliefs.'

Whatever I have said is solely from the standpoint of the needs of the Ahmadiyya Jamā'at and from its religious perspective. As for what course of action others should adopt, or under what rules and principles one should take part in politics—provided it is not harmful to get involved in it—that is a separate debate. At this time, it is not necessary to speak on this subject. For the time being, it is sufficient to say that the present needs of Islam require our Jamā'at to stay away from politics. Our Jamā'at should not involve itself in politics even to the extent readily allowed by the government. On the contrary, our members should spend all their time to accomplish the task which God has assigned to them. They must not let their attention be diverted, nor should they risk spoiling their character by indulging in politics.

Marriage between Aḥmadīs and non-Aḥmadīs and Issue of Kufw[4]

The third important issue that I wish to discuss today is the question of Aḥmadīs marrying non-Aḥmadīs. This issue also brings into question parity between marital partners. I have always been aware of the problems which our Jamā'at has faced with regards to

[4] *Kufw*, which is one of the desired considerations in an Islamic marriage, literally means likeness and equality of tribe, caste or family. It may roughly be rendered as 'economic and social compatibility.'

performing the important custom of marriage. But over a period of about last nine months, I have come to know about a number of problems and hurdles which Aḥmadīs are facing with regards to performing this important ritual. From the letters written to me by the members of the Jamā'at, I understand that people are under a lot of stress due to the prevailing situation. The Promised Messiah[as] had also planned to put down the names of all the Ahmadi boys and girls in a register. He ordered for a register to be opened at some member's request who had submitted to him that people face a lot of difficulty when it comes to marrying their sons or daughters, and keeping in view the directive of the Promised Messiah[as], matrimonial relationships could not be established with non-Aḥmadīs. He wrote that Aḥmadīs were living at scattered places. He sought the guidance of the Promised Messiah[as] in this regard and suggested that there should be a register where the names of all the unmarried Ahmadi boys and girls are properly recorded, so that the marriages were easily arranged. He said that in this way the Promised Messiah[as], when requested, would himself be able to propose some possible matches with the help of that register. He said that there was no Ahmadi who could disobey the choice of the Promised Messiah[as].

Unfortunately, some people give suggestions due to their own selfish desires. It seems, in this case too, the intention of the man giving the suggestion for the register was not upright. There was a sincere and pious Ahmadi who wanted to get married. The man who had forwarded the idea of making up of a register happened to have a daughter. The Promised Messiah[as] told the Ahmadi in need of marriage to enquire from the said person if he was interested. The man rejected the proposal and refused to give away his daughter to him after putting forth some lame excuse. Later, he married his daughter to a non-Ahmadi. When the Promised Messiah[as] came to learn of it, he said that he wouldn't involve himself in such issues any more. So, the proposal of a register did not move forward. Had a register been opened at that time, Aḥmadīs may not have faced as much of trouble as they are facing today.

Marriage is Essential

It is essential for every nation, if they wish to survive and prosper in the world, to maintain the institution of marriage. This is also the decree of God regarding this institution. The Holy Prophet[sa] has stated that all believers should marry, and that one who dies unmarried, dies a death of ignorance; but Aḥmadīs are faced with a number of problems in following this important injunction. The reason is that the relationship with non-Aḥmadīs is not so amicable, so as a result they refuse to give their daughters in marriage to them. People living in the same village sometimes marry their daughters off to people living in the same village, and so that their daughters won't have to go outside the village. But Aḥmadīs are not confined to one single place. They are scattered in distances apart from each other. Moreover, their numbers are also very small. Therefore, if they marry their daughters only to Aḥmadīs, they have to send them to far off places. The condition and culture of those living far away has to be carefully examined. Those related to the boy are curious about the habits and physical features of the girl; whereas, those related to the girl want the boy to be of some good standing if they have to send their daughter to a remote place. This causes a delay in the marriage resulting in additional problems. Moreover, one has to carefully monitor their own household in case daughters have to stay at home for some time and wait to get married—just because of the hostile social environment surrounding the family in such cases. As for other people they may not be so conscious of this problem, but we are, because we have been raised to reform the world. In short, Aḥmadīs are faced with many problems regarding the issue of marriage. At times, those who are weak of faith fail to practice restraint and marry their daughters to non-Aḥmadīs. This is a source of great distress for me, for marrying our girls to non-Aḥmadīs causes much damage. What is more, such a *nikāḥ* [the announcement of marriage in Islam] in itself is not permissible. Since women are naturally weak and not always properly trained, they tend to adopt the ways and beliefs of the family they get married into which then destroys their own faith. And if they remain firm in their beliefs, there is always going to be perpetual conflict between them and their husbands, for the difference of beliefs will then ruin the love that should exist between a husband and wife. This deprives them of peace and comfort of heart. Then there are times when a person, in order to show that he is fully obeying the command of the Promised Messiah[as], spreads the news that the person to whom he is going to marry his daughters is an Ahmadi or someone that has recently joined the Jamā'at. He says that only the formal initiation remains, and that such a person will pledge bai'at as soon as he is able to visit Qadian. They also get him to write a letter [for *bai'at*]. In certain cases, such a person even turns up in Qadian and pledges *bai'at*. In certain other cases, boys, in order to get the hand of a girl of their choice, deceive the girl's family by saying that they have already written a letter pledging their *bai'at*, thereby demanding that the family of the girl should marry their daughter to him. But *nikāḥs* of this kind never result in true happiness, for the intention behind them is not good. God does not need a person who enters the Jamā'at only for the sake of marriage. Nor does such a person stay steadfast with his pledge of *bai'at*, or change his way of life to adopt better morals. Even if he sticks to his pledge of *bai'at*, he proves to be a constant source of annoyance for the Jamā'at. There have been a number of such incidents and their result has always been undesirable. At times, it was bad from the religious point of view and at times from the worldly point of view. There have been some exceptions as well, but they are very few indeed. In most cases, husbands start tormenting their wives once the *nikāḥ* has been solemnized, and force them to relinquish their religious beliefs. At times, they stop them from offering prayers or even reciting the Holy Quran. A few years back, I came to know of a man who had married his daughter to a person who had become an Ahmadi only for the sake of marriage. The family of that person began torturing the bride in various ways. When she performed *Ṣalāt*, she was accused by them of practicing some magic; and of doing some magical tricks against the family when she recited the Holy Quran. That poor girl was rendered unable to offer prayers or recite the Holy Quran. Her father became extremely worried and started looking for some solution. But how could someone help him? It was the punishment of his own action that he was receiving. Another person wrote to me that he had married his daughter to a non-Ahmadi. His daughter's husband insisted that he will neither keep her as a wife, nor will he divorce her, and that instead he will keep disturbing her family and be a constant source of worry for them.

In short, those who marry their daughters to non-Aḥmadīs can never be at peace. By doing this, they actually destroy the faith of their daughters, and this is something for which they will surely be held accountable [in the sight of Allah]. In addition, they themselves keep feeling the agony of their action. For those who, despite being believers, marry their daughters to mere world-seeker, can never live in peace, and neither can their daughters ever find true happiness. Whereas if someone marries his daughter to even the poorest Ahmadi, he will have saved his daughter from losing her faith. A very strict command of the Promised Messiah[as] is that no Ahmadi should marry his daughter to a non-Ahmadi. Therefore, it is incumbent upon every Ahmadi to follow this guidance. To follow the command of the Promised Messiah[as], it is also essential to follow the system adopted by the Jamā'at in this regard. There is no doubt that the Jamā'at will have to make a lot of sacrifices in order to follow this command. The Aḥmadīs should marry their daughters when they have found a faithful and pious person—regardless of whether or not he is well-off. Do people not marry their daughters to relatives who are comparatively less fortunate than them? They do! The point I wish to make is: who is nearer and dearer to Aḥmadīs than the people of their own faith? This spiritual relationship is far more important than any other affiliation or relationship. Therefore, you should shun the old and rotten customs, and try to marry your daughters when you have found a pious and righteous person for them.

Problem of Tribal and Family Considerations

Another problem in marriages is the tribal background. I am in favour of parity. The Promised Messiah[as] also stressed upon observing it. But there are limits for everything, and it is generally advisable to stay within those limits. Parity means a person matching one's own living standard, way of life, morals, and, of course, piety and righteousness. For instance, should a rich man give away his daughter to a poor and famished person, it may be wise and appropriate as far as religion is concerned, but once the girl reaches her husband's house the couple will have confrontations and disagreements with each other, for the girl will not get as much money to spend as she was used to. That is why it is important for every father to look for a person of similar position as compared to himself, so that the husband and wife do not keep on getting into disagreements due to the austerity; or so that the girl should not consider herself to be a victim of cruelty and unkindness. However, one should not be so overwhelmed with this precaution that everyone should start wishing to have his daughter married to the wealthiest man on earth, for then it would become impossible for the girls of the poor families to get married. Everyone should consider his own position first. If there is a proposed match in which the difference is tolerable, one should not hesitate to proceed with it. Complications arise only where differences are intolerable, as for example the marriage of the daughter of a rich man to a person who cannot even feed her satisfactorily even two times a day.

In the same vein, it would be wrong on the part of a person who himself has no material comforts but desires his daughter to marry some high official. He should rather marry his daughter to a simple and pious person whose social standing is similar to his own. There are some people with the same mentality in our Jamā'at. Someone once requested Ḥaḍrat Khalīfatul-Masīḥ I to look for and arrange the marriage of his daughter or sister, but when Ḥaḍrat Khalīfatul-Masīḥ I proposed some names to him, he turned them down saying they were not really worth the girl. He said that she rather deserved to be married to some Tehsildar, Extra Assistant Commissioner or a person of another equally respectable position. This was in spite of the fact that the person himself was of a very ordinary standing. Such behaviour can create serious problems for those who are not so fortunate. A non-Ahmadi would give his daughter to an Ahmadi only when he is sure that the Ahmadi is fairly better placed than him. After all, why would he give away his daughter to an Ahmadi if he does not gain any material benefit from that relationship? There are exceptions, albeit very few. The poor are not going to find any match [for their children] from among the non-Aḥmadīs. Now, what they are left with are only the people of their own faith. If they start behaving with arrogance, it will create a major problem for a certain portion of the Jamā'at.

The point of my saying all this is not that one should turn down the offer of a good match, and insist that he would like to marry his daughter only when he finds a person of meagre resources equal to his own. Rather, one must not be ungrateful to God if God extends His grace upon him. To me it is wrong to delay the marriages of girls in the hope of finding some rich person for them. Marry them once you have found for them someone who you think has a fairly good income and is pious, but should you fail to find a person of this sort and have an offer from someone who is equal to you in status or has circumstances which fairly match yours—and is not guilty of any misconduct—you must not reject him simply due to the pretext of his financial position. The effort to look for someone who is earning a lot of money and is very rich by someone who himself is only earning a hundred rupees per month results in great trouble, because having failed to find their desired match among Aḥmadīs, they tend to marry their girls to non-Aḥmadīs. Abstaining from such a wrong and ridiculous way of searching for suitable partners, every Ahmadi should look for a person of his own status so that the girls do not suffer, and to prevent them from having to be married to non-Aḥmadīs. There had also been a tradition among some respected families to arrange for the everyday expenditure of both the husband [their son-in-law] and the wife once they found that the husband, though not so fortunate and well-off, was righteous and God-fearing. It would indeed be commendable if some were able to follow the same tradition even today. Should that seem impossible to follow, one should look for a person of his own standing and position. As I have stated earlier, I consider the worldly status of a person to be an important consideration when it comes to parity, and as I have just mentioned, I do believe that it should be given due consideration.

The second question which is to be discussed under the subject of parity is the family background. Family background too has to be considered to some extent. In fact, it is a natural consideration. For instance, if a person of a noble family gives away his daughter to a man who has converted into Islam from the sweeper community, the daughter would consider her husband to be of low-birth. Their relationship will result in a permanent discord between them, and the very purpose of marriage will remain unfulfilled. Or should there be some other flaw making a wife consider her husband to be inferior to her or vice versa, their relationship will be fraught with constant discord.

That is why one should always keep in mind that there should never be such a stark difference between a husband and wife as far as their habits are concerned or their education or social standing. Such differences always become a bone of contention between partners. The tribal differences also have taken root due to the same problems. There is no harm in giving one's daughter to a person who belongs to a respectable tribe and is engaged in a respectable business. Just reflect about which family the Promised Messiah[as] married his daughter into! He did not give her away to someone from among the Mughals. Nor are any of our brothers married into Mughal families. Even I, who have married a second time, have not married a Mughal. The point I wish to make is that one should take into account a person's righteousness and good manners. Only that family is noble which practices good morals and observes social decencies. A Sayyed who is ignorant of his religious obligations is not noble. The Holy Quran has beautifully illustrated its point regarding the existence of various tribes and castes. It states:[5]

يَآأَيُّهَا النَّاسُ إِنَّا خَلَقْنٰكُمْ مِّنْ ذَكَرٍ وَّأُنْثٰى وَجَعَلْنٰكُمْ شُعُوْبًا وَّقَبَآئِلَ
لِتَعَارَفُوْا ؕ إِنَّ أَكْرَمَكُمْ عِنْدَ اللّٰهِ أَتْقٰكُمْ ؕ إِنَّ اللّٰهَ عَلِيْمٌ خَبِيْرٌ ﴿١٤﴾

---

[5] O mankind, We have created you from a male and a female; and We have made you into tribes and sub-tribes that you may recognize one another. Verily, the most honourable among you, in the sight of Allah, is he who is the most righteous among you. Surely, Allah is All-knowing, All-Aware. (*Sūrah al-Ḥujurāt 49:14)*

That is, God Almighty says: O people! We have created you from one man and one woman. If this means from Adam and Eve, then what precedence can you claim to have over each other for, after all, you have been born out of the same father and mother. Therefore, you can never claim superiority over each other. The second meaning could be that all of you, without exception, have been born of one woman. All have been born in the same way. Similarly, all have been born of someone's seminal fluid. How can you then claim precedence over one another? In this part of the verse, God has turned down the unjustified claim of precedence by anyone and has declared all to be one. Hence, one has no right to claim supremacy over another.

Again, the Holy Quran says:[6]

...جَعَلْنٰكُمْ شُعُوْبًا وَّ قَبَآئِلَ...

That is: We have divided you into different nations and tribes. This part of the verse explains that tribes and nations also are of some importance. In the next part of the verse God says: لِتَعَارَفُوْا that is, the purpose of the division into nations and tribes is not that they should take pride over each other or consider others to be inferior to you. Rather, the only purpose of this division is so that they can identify and recognize one another. This is like governments dividing their armies and other departments into different categories. In a system where there are so many people working, one has to find some way to identify each other. It was to meet this particular requirement that people were divided into different clans

6 *Ibid.*

and tribes. Almighty God also has drawn the attention of the people towards the point that this is the only reason why people have been divided into different tribes and castes.

Look at the governments that have large armies. They first divide them into divisions, and then to distinguish between them, they give them different names. Then they divide them further into regiments and platoons and companies. The purpose of all these divisions is to achieve efficiency and help facilitate recognition to one other. For instance, should we say that such and such a person is a soldier in the government army, our saying so does not clarify where the said person lives or where his company or regiment has camped; but if we say he belongs to such and such platoon, and lives in a specific cantonment, he can be located quickly. The tribes, too, have their names for the same purpose. However, these divisions also make it clear that not all people are alike. Some are more noble and decent, while some happen to be less noble and decent, and then some drop down even further. There is definitely going to be difference, but who is really noble? To explain this, the Holy Quran says:[7]

...اِنَّ اَكْرَمَكُمْ عِنْدَ اللّٰهِ اَتْقٰكُمْ ...

That is: The most honourable among you in the sight of Allah, is he who is more pious, or who is more righteous and God-fearing. The more one fears Allah, the more righteous and pious he becomes. This has been clearly illustrated that there are people who are good, and there are those who are not good. The noble are those who are

---

7 *Ibid.*

noble in the sight of God and are considered righteous by Him. Therefore, it is wrong to marry a noble person to an ignoble one. This is exactly in accordance with the divine injunction where God Almighty says:[8]

اَلزَّانِيْ لَا يَنْكِحُ اِلَّا زَانِيَةً اَوْ مُشْرِكَةً ۫ وَّ الزَّانِيَةُ لَا يَنْكِحُهَاۤ اِلَّا زَانٍ
اَوْ مُشْرِكٌ ۚ وَحُرِّمَ ذٰلِكَ عَلَى الْمُؤْمِنِيْنَ ۝

That is: It is indeed difficult for a noble person to be the companion of a depraved person. Ḥaḍrat Khalīfatul-Masīḥ I[ra] used to narrate that a man used to visit a prostitute and ignored his wife. One day, his wife called a prostitute and asked her why husbands would leave their wives and visit prostitutes instead. She said that prostitutes entice their clients through coquetry. When a man approaches them, they push him away with their legs and do not let him get near. They also coax him and playfully cajole him. This provides pleasure to an evil person and makes him fall in love with them even more. Having learned this, one day when her husband returned, she started hurling abuses at him. When he came nearer, she gave him a couple of slaps as well. He was completely aghast at what was happening. He knew her to be an obedient woman who had never misbehaved with him. He felt utterly shocked since he failed to understand the reason for her misbehaviour. But then he realized what had gone wrong and confessed his mistake. But the

---

8 The adulterer (or fornicator) shall not marry but an adulteress (or fornicatress) or an idolatrous woman, and an adulteress (or fornicatress) shall not marry but an adulterer (or fornicator) or an idolatrous man. That indeed is forbidden to the believers. (*Sūrah an-Nūr*, 24:4)

woman's anger had not yet subsided when she taunted him saying 'you fall for that filth and do not turn towards an obedient wife'.

In short, it is an established fact that a depraved person falls for a depraved woman and a depraved woman falls for a depraved man. Likewise, pious women and men give preference to what is pure and chaste, and all their relationships are built accordingly. Their subsistence depends on this principle, for two things cannot coexist unless there is a binding similarity between them. Ḥaḍrat Muhyud-Dīn Ibni Arabi[rh] says that once he saw a crow and dove sitting together. It surprised him since he failed to find any similarity between them that could bring them together. He decided to sit and wait. After a while, when the other birds had left, he came to know that both of them were unable to walk evenly. Ḥaḍrat Muhyud-Dīn Ibni Arabi said that it was this similarity which made them sit together. Therefore, it is important for every man and woman to share some common values and possess some common attributes. Birds of a feather are said to flock together. A relationship can succeed only when both the man and woman share some commonalities. A noble person will surely suffer a great deal if he is married to an immoral person. How serious would the suffering be of a poor Ahmadi girl if she is married to a person who is simply unaware of his religion, does not even offer prayers, and is ignorant of the other religious obligations? Will she be able to lead a happy life? Never! A *hadith* says if a woman does not turn up when her husband calls her for marital relations, she is cursed the whole night. So referencing this *hadith*, there has been so much stress laid upon the obedience of a wife towards her husband, but if there is a confrontation between them, will this situation not cause the woman to suffer? How on earth can such a household remain peaceful?

Verdict of the Holy Prophet About Status

The Holy Prophet[sa] was indeed so graceful in his manner of speech that those possessed of pious nature cannot help but dearly fall in love with him. Since Arabs were very particular about family backgrounds and genealogies, they asked the Holy Prophet[sa] who among them was the most noble. They expected the Holy Prophet[sa] to name some tribes, thereby causing those who named to be considered more respectable by others. The Holy Prophet[sa] answered that the best among them was the one who was pious and God-fearing. They submitted, 'O Prophet of Allah! Our question was not meant to ask about this.' The Holy Prophet[sa] then said, 'Well, then the most noble was Joseph, since he himself was a Prophet, and so was his father and grandfather.' All praise is due to Allah. How beautifully he answered the question raised by his companions! They were provided with an answer, yet at the same time, no one's feelings were hurt. They submitted, 'O Prophet of Allah! Of course we did not mean this either.' The Holy Prophet[sa] said, 'Well, maybe your question regards the tribes of Arabia. Hearken! The same who were considered worthy of respect during the age of ignorance, are also worthy of respect and noble in Islam. The only condition is that they must be well acquainted with their religion.'

The *hadith* goes as thus:

عن ابی ہریرۃ رضی اللّٰہ عنہ قال سئل رسول اللّٰہ صلی اللّٰہ علیہ
وسلم من اکرم الناس قال اتقاھم للّٰہ قالوا لیس عن ھذا نسالک
قال فاکرم الناس یوسف نبی اللّٰہ ابن نبی اللّٰہ ابن نبی اللّٰہ ابن خلیل
اللّٰہ قالوا لیس عن ھذا نسالک قال فعن معادن العرب تسالونی
الناس معادن خیارھم فی الجاھلیۃ خیارھم فی الاسلام اذا فقھوا

Ḥaḍrat Abu Hurairah[ra] relates that once the Holy Prophet[sa] was asked about who was the noblest among people. The Holy Prophet[sa] said, 'He who fears Allah more than others, is nobler than others.' The companions of the Holy Prophet[sa] submitted, 'O Prophet of Allah! Our question was not meant to ask about that.' The Holy Prophet[sa] said, 'Then Joseph is the best since he himself was a Prophet; his father was a Prophet; and his grandfather was *Khalīlullāh*, the friend of Allah.' The companions of the Holy Prophet[sa] submitted again, 'We did not mean to ask about that.' At this the Holy Prophet[sa] enquired if they were asking about different tribes and nations of Arabia. Well, in that case, he said, 'Hearken that people are divided into different tribes. [Or he said that they were like mines.] The same among them, who were considered to be noble during the pre-Islamic period, will be considered to be noble in Islam as well, provided they have solid knowledge of their religion.'

In the course of this question and answer session, the Holy Prophet[sa] has thrice answered the question raised by his companions. Should one reflect, it is clear that all three answers are in fact the same. Although, he changed his words a little, the overall conclusion remained the same. In the first instance, he said that the one who is the most pious is the noblest. Secondly, he declared Joseph to be the noblest inasmuch as he was a Prophet and the son of a Prophet and the grandson of yet another Prophet. In other words, because he himself was of a pious nature, the son of a pious person, and the grandson of yet another pious person, he was then the noblest. Answering it in this way also, he connected nobility with righteousness. Lastly, he kept the same point in view when he answered the question the third time. He said that those who were considered to be noble in the pre-Islamic period would also be considered noble after they have become Muslims, provided they develop true understanding of their religion. Becoming conversant with one's religion is indeed a great virtue. To learn a religion is different from having its true understanding and being conversant with its true philosophy. True understanding requires that a person should come to know about the true spirit and philosophy of the teachings his religion has to offer. By applying this condition, the Holy Prophet[sa] has again indicated that noble is he who is righteous, God-fearing and possesses a true understanding of the faith. In short, all three answers have illustrated for Muslims the true sense of nobility in a beautiful way so that they do not consider it linked to only one's family background, and so that they continue making efforts to attain nearness to Allah. These answers have made it absolutely clear that the one who does not practice righteousness—be he of any nation or tribe—cannot be called noble, for nobility requires him to be pious and God-fearing.

Criterion of a Noble Family

The criterion of a noble family and the reason why certain families can be called noble has also been expounded in the previously mentioned verse of the Holy Quran and saying of the Holy Prophet[sa]. Sayyeds, for example, are considered to be the noblest of castes among the Muslims. The reason for that is obvious. They are related to the most righteous of the Muslims—the Holy Prophet[sa].

Why do Brahmins hold the highest position among the Hindus and why they are considered to be the noblest of families? It was for no reason other than that they taught religion to others and also acted upon it themselves. Thus they became the highest and most respected among the castes on the basis of the same principle of[9]

...إِنَّ أَكْرَمَكُمْ عِنْدَ اللّٰهِ أَتْقٰكُمْ ...

Those doing menial jobs in the world are considered to be of the lowest origin, and this is due their keeping themselves among lowly things which consequently affects their morals and habits as well. It is according to this principle that people have held certain tribes and families to be of high in status or low. For instance, there is a caste of shoemakers. There was a time when this profession held no importance, and most of their dealings were with families similar to

[9] Verily, the most honourable among you, in the sight of Allah, is he who is the most righteous among you. (*Sūrah al-Ḥujurāt*, 49:14)

theirs. People of high descent would not even visit their shops in person. Moreover, they would not invest very large sums of money in their businesses, and so their shops would be rather small. Gradually, it was for this reason that people started ranking them among the castes which were considered to be lowly in society. Of course it was a natural outcome of their being always in touch with people who were also considered to be in low classes.

On the other hand, the shoemakers of England do this business with large sums of money and have relations with people of high social standing. That is why their condition has changed and people consider them to be among the respectable, for the moral deprivation that was feared because of their particular circumstances is no longer a threat.

Similarly, there are professions which naturally cast an ill-effect on anyone involved with them. Take for example music, which—without anyone's being involved in any other kind of unacceptable relationship—casts an adverse influences on the heart of the person involved. That is why those related to this profession are considered to be of low status.

As you will witness, families that have emerged as noble have achieved that status due to righteousness, piety and good morals. Some tribes became respectable because they were related to some pious person, some because of being related to someone who was indeed very brave and some because of their relationship with some great conqueror. Should we take a look at the roots of some nations, their nobility would be found to have resulted from their being possessed of good morals at some time in the past, and since the relationships that man takes do affect his morals, it becomes necessary to some extent to take into consideration the element of nobility in people. It is therefore important to observe a nation's good and bad traits, so that one does not have to suffer indignation or embarrassment at some later stage.

Morals are observed for the sake of achieving good results. Should someone manage to find a young man who has a way of life similar to his own—be he of any tribe or caste—he should settle for the match. One, who is considered to be ignoble today, can become noble tomorrow. Should someone convert from a lowly position—for instance, a sweeper—and become Muslim, I can dine with him right away. I can eat from what he has eaten and he from what I have eaten, for there remains no difference between me and him when he has said:[10]

لاالہ الاالله محمد رسول الله

According to Islam, he must enjoy the same rights as I do, and there shall be no distinction, whatsoever.

A king who had converted to Islam during the reign of Ḥaḍrat Umar[ra] came [to visit Makkah]. While he was performing circuits of the Ka'abah, a garment of his came under the feet of some companion of the Holy Prophet[sa]. The king slapped the companion. At this, somebody told the king that Ḥaḍrat Umar[ra] would surely avenge the companion. The king was surprised and said, 'Will he take revenge from me, the king of Ghassan, for the sake of that pauper, and will he not relent even me?' He was told, 'No!' Having become even more concerned, he went to see Ḥaḍrat

---

[10] There is none worthy of worship except Allah; Muhammad is the Messenger of Allah.

Umar[ra] in person and submitted, 'If a person of little standing were to get beaten by someone of high standing, you would not avenge the person of low status, would you?' Ḥaḍrat Umar[ra] said, 'I hope you have not beaten anybody up! If you have been guilty of hitting someone, I will, by God, surely avenge the person.' Having heard this, the king fled by the night and all his countrymen converted to Christianity. When Ḥaḍrat Umar[ra] came to know of this, he said, 'we do not need such people.'

Therefore, as far as rights are concerned, all Muslims are equal. But that is not the only thing to be considered when it comes to marriages. One also has to observe whether there exist too many differences between the persons who are going to be tied to other for the rest of their lives. People of certain nations are, by nature, ill-mannered. They should be avoided as life partners in order to put off permanent conflict. In view of keeping the peaceful living between the boy and the girl, parity too will have to be given due consideration. But as I have already said there is a limit to everything. By saying that God has set out the principle that true nobility lies in true righteousness, one should not call people of a particular caste to be absolutely base or of low-birth. You may avoid being in relationships with them, but you must not call anyone base or mean; for the one who is noble today, can become base tomorrow due to changing circumstances. All are equal in the sight of Allah. Only he is superior who shows an upright and virtuous character. If the moral character and habits of a man as are different from the values of the family of the girl, they should not be forced to marry. But to impose the condition that the person should belong only to the clan of Mughals—not only that, but that he should also descend from the Barlas tribe of the Mughals—should certainly not happen. In marriages, you should first consider a person's piety and good character. The issue of parity comes later and that too should be taken into account to the extent of certain family values relating to the person's cultural and moral backgrounds. You must remember that to fulfil your obligations, a lot of sacrifices are to be made on your part. Though an Ahmadi is permitted to take in marriage the daughter of a non-Ahmadi for his son, our circumstances are such that they require that the members of the Jamā'at should neither give their daughters to non-Aḥmadīs, nor should they take daughters of non-Aḥmadīs for their sons. The initial directive that the Promised Messiah[as] had given in this regard carried this same judgment that Aḥmadīs should establish marital relations only with other Aḥmadīs. Only later did he grant permission for Ahmadi males to marry into non-Ahmadi families. Now the circumstances have taken such a turn that once again it seems appropriate that Aḥmadīs should neither give away their daughters to the non-Aḥmadīs, nor should they take the daughters of non-Aḥmadīs in marriage for their sons except in very dire circumstances. I say so because at this time the number of people in our Jamā'at is very small and the difficulty which the Jamā'at is facing is that because Ahmadi boys do get married to non-Ahmadi girls, and since Ahmadi girls are not being allowed to get married to non-Aḥmadīs, it becomes difficult to locate a match for them from among Aḥmadīs. This consequently makes some Aḥmadīs show their weakness of faith, for they then give their daughters away to non-Ahmadi boys. There are so many people who write to me for help regarding the arrangement for the marriages of their daughters. When I look towards the male members of our Jamā'at, I find them already married into non-Ahmadi families. The point I wish to make is that if Ahmadi boys continue to get married into non-Ahmadi families, what will happen of the Ahmadi girls? Do you think it is a viable proposition in any way that Ahmadi girls should be married to non-Aḥmadīs and undergo hardships? Only that Jamā'at can survive which looks after the well-being of all of its members. Considering the circumstances the Jamā'at is facing today, you should avoid taking non-Ahmadi girls into marriages [for Ahmadi boys], so as to protect your people against trials and hardships and so that you continue to grow stronger as a Jamā'at.

Prayer in Congregation

There is another flaw to which I wish to draw your attention. Some flaws may appear to be minor in the beginning, but become serious with the passage of time and cause great damage. There is a flaw in our Jamā'at—and I know that it is due to the circumstances faced by a part of the members. But every Ahmadi is required to be extremely vigilant. If we do not attend to it and do not find ways to set it straight, it may result in great harm for the Jamā'at and result in very serious consequences. That flaw is concerning the offering of congregational prayer.

There is no doubt that Aḥmadīs are faced with a problem in this regard in that they cannot offer prayers behind non-Aḥmadīs, and there are many places where only one Ahmadi lives. He, therefore, finds himself unable to offer prayers in congregation. One has to be punctual for offering prayers in congregation, and so it happens that slowly having failed to be on time for prayers due to not having to say them in congregation, one starts showing slackness and tends to think that he can offer them at a time of his choice. This makes him unmindful of the importance of being on time for prayers, eventually causing him to lose the habit of offering prayers on time. Such a person often gets into the habit of combining the prayers, and becomes so oblivious to offering them in congregation that even if there are times when he has a chance to offer prayers in congregation, he does not do so. It is true that he takes to this habit due to unavoidable circumstances, but Aḥmadīs should make sure that they never show slackness in regard to the offering of prayers. No sooner will this slackness take over the Jamā'at than the journey towards destruction will start. May Allah protect us against such an outcome.

So where there is only one Ahmadi in a village, he should try to convert one more person to Aḥmadiyyat. Should he do this, I hope, God will provide him with a companion in faith. But in case he fails to find a companion he should go to some other village every second or third day and offer his prayers in congregation. Don't let laziness overtake you. Remember that if you forget this advice of mine, you will never prosper.

It poses a great difficulty for Aḥmadīs who live in big cities and who find it hard to visit their fellows to always be together for prayers. Therefore, what they should do is congregate with the people in their own area on certain occasions and offer prayers in congregation. You should never allow slackness to overcome you. This is such a dangerous thing and brings about horrible consequences. What I have understood from the Holy Quran is that if one is able to offer prayers in congregation but does not do so, he simply has not offered any prayers.

It is hard to put in words how careful the Holy Prophet[sa] was about not missing any of the congregational prayers. Once a blind person came to him and submitted to him that it was very difficult for him to come to the mosque, and that there was nobody who could hold his hand and help him to the mosque. He submitted if he could be permitted to offer the prayers at home. The Holy Prophet[sa] granted him the permission. But when he was about to leave, the Holy Prophet[sa] called him back and asked if he could hear the call for the prayers while at his home. He said that he could hear the call. At this, the Holy Prophet[sa] said, 'If the call for prayer reaches your place, you should come to the mosque to offer the prayers.'

In order to further lay stress on this point, the Holy Prophet[sa] went as far as saying that he wished he could ask someone else to stand in his place to lead the prayer, and then take some of his companions with loads of firewood on their heads and burn down the houses of those who do not show up for the congregational prayers, thus destroying both the houses and the occupants. Behold, the Holy Prophet[sa] was gracious, noble, kind and beneficent, and yet he wished the houses of those who habitually missed congregational prayers to be burnt down. Surely, this *hadith* manifestly illustrates the significance of offering prayers in congregation.

He specified the Prayers of *'Ishā* and *Fajr;* the reason is that these two times pose a greater difficulty for a believer. At the time of the *'Ishā* Prayer people show laziness because they are sleepy and in the morning because they find it hard to get up. Considering that the Holy Prophet[sa] expressed such great concern about these two times, the emphasis upon offering the other prayers in congregation also becomes very obvious. The truth is that a Jamā'at can never be established unless it pays due attention to offering prayers in congregation. That is why you should strive as hard as possible to make it incumbent upon yourselves to offer prayers in congregation. Should someone fail to find a companion to accompany him for congregation, he can arrange for congregation at home leading the prayers while his wife and children stand behind him. This will at least keep the habit of offering prayers in congregation alive. A day will come that God will make that single person into a full-fledged Jamā'at. May Allah enable you all to fulfil your obligation in this regard.

Zakat

Zakat is another important issue. People have failed to fully grasp the ideology behind it. God has commanded this after the Prayer. Ḥaḍrat Abu Bakr[ra] said, 'I will deal with those who do not pay Zakat like the Holy Prophet[sa] dealt with the disbelievers. I will enslave their men and take their women as servants.' After the demise of the Holy Prophet[sa], the whole of Arabia had turned apostate with the exception of only three cities; namely, Makkah, Madinah, and another one. At that time, Ḥaḍrat Umar[ra] submitted to Ḥaḍrat Abu Bakr[ra] that in view of the riots that had broken throughout the country the expedition which was supposed to leave for Syria should be halted. But the answer given by Ḥaḍrat Abu Bakr[ra] was that he could not halt the expedition whose departure had been commanded by the Holy Prophet[sa] himself. Then Ḥaḍrat

Umar[ra] proposed to reconcile with those who had declined to pay Zakat. He was of the view that such people would gradually get reformed and that the war should first be waged against the other apostates. He thought that the need of the hour was to crush the false claimants of Prophethood, since they were the source of the greatest trouble. The answer that Ḥaḍrat Abu Bakr[ra] gave on this occasion was that if people do not pay that much Zakat that they used to pay to the Holy Prophet[sa]—even if it be so small an amount as the young of a goat or a rope to tie the camels—he would wage war against them, and that he would fight against them alone if all others abandoned him and the beasts of jungle attacked him accompanied by every single person who recanted.

In short, Ḥaḍrat Abu Bakr[ra] ascribed so much importance to the injunction of Zakat that he thought it absolutely wise to treat its defaulter like a disbeliever. Alas, there are just a few among the Muslims who give serious attention to it. I have estimated that if we calculate the Zakat which is paid by the Ahmadiyya Jamā'at, it amounts to around a hundred thousand rupees. This is because almost everyone possesses some amount of gold these days. The Promised Messiah[as] has said that the things on which the government levies tax do not fall under the articles on which Zakat is to be paid, since the government already collects tax on them. But I am of the view that the tax that the government levies on agricultural land is less than the amount that has been fixed by the Shariah. Therefore, where government tax is less than the amount fixed by the Shariah, the concerned person must pay the remaining amount as Zakat. For instance, should government collect land revenue [of five rupees] for a part of land in somebody's possession whose one-tenth portion amounts to ten rupees, the owner is under the obligation to send five rupees as tithe here [to Qadian]. In order to arrange for this collection, the secretaries of the Ahmadiyya Anjumans in every village and town should start making registers wherein they should record all the items of jewellery and other items on which Zakat is obligatory, and make sure that the amount is collected regularly. In cases where a secretary is not available to do so, somebody else should arrange for the register.

The Promised Messiah[as] has said that it is not obligatory to pay Zakat on the items of jewellery that are in regular use of a person; but if someone volunteers some contribution it would certainly be appreciated. One must pay Zakat on items not in regular use, and I have already directed the publishing of a detailed booklet covering all the rules and regulations regarding Zakat. It should be properly followed and put into practice.

Benefits of Zakat

The injunction of Zakat is indeed an unprecedented one and is one of the innumerable and extraordinary excellences of Islam. It is one that can truly and conclusively establish the glory of Islam over all other religions. Take Europe as the example, where two new groups have emerged recently. One of them is of the opinion that everyone should have the right to earn as much as he can and enjoy the fruit of his labour. The other one is of the view that wealth is generated only when everyone living in a country goes to work. For this reason, they say money should be taken away from those who have plenty of wealth at their disposal and should be distributed among the poor and the deprived so that they do not die of hunger, and the enterprise of the state does not suffer decline or recession. God has set forth what is most upright and best, and putting aside the extreme positions, has given the middle way that is the best. I firmly believe that should one put forth only the system of Zakat before Europe, no one will be able to find any excuse to deny the sublime qualities and excellences of this system.

There are people who consider Zakat to be a kind of penalty, whereas it is not a penalty at all. To help you understand this, I will give a simple example. The government collects tax from its citizens, and then from that tax it builds the army and police to protect the country and its people. In order to bring comfort to its subjects, the government constructs roads and hospitals and provides the population with numerous benefits. Since the government collects a tax with the intent of providing facilities for its citizens, nobody considers such a tax to be a penalty. Similarly, Zakat is not a penalty; rather, the injunction in this regard has been issued in the interest of the people themselves. Just as a government collects tax for the betterment of its citizens, God too has imposed Zakat and has promised that as a recompense of this payment your fortunes will be blessed greatly and that they will become secure against every kind of loss and misfortune. God says:[11]

خُذْ مِنْ اَمْوَالِهِمْ صَدَقَةً تُطَهِّرُهُمْ وَتُزَكِّيْهِمْ بِهَا وَصَلِّ عَلَيْهِمْ ۗ اِنَّ
صَلٰوتَكَ سَكَنٌ لَّهُمْ ۗ وَاللّٰهُ سَمِيْعٌ عَلِيْمٌ ﴿۱۰۳﴾

That is: Take alms out of their wealth, so that you may cleanse them and purify them thereby. And pray for them, because your

---

[11] *Sūrah at-Taubah*, 9:103

prayers are a source of comfort and tranquillity for them. [And Allah is All-Hearing, All-Knowing].

In short, Zakat is a tax imposed by God on man in return for which He has promised to bless him with physical and spiritual purity. Ever since the Muslims have stopped paying Zakat, they are observing a constant decline in their wealth. Alas, there was a time when they ruled the whole world, but today they are afflicted with adversity and abasement. God promises worldly success and spiritual purity to those who pay Zakat, in the same way as a government promises protection in return for the tax it collects from its subjects. But alas, people give credence to the promises made by a worldly government and happily pay all taxes, whereas they deny the truth of the promise made by God, thereby declining to pay Zakat. The fact is that, as a consequence of paying Zakat, one becomes secure from a number of problems and miseries, for divine promises can never be false.

A Subtle Point About Zakat

Among the many great advantages of Zakat, there is one which may prove beneficial particularly to those with a Sufi nature. When a man is earning his living he makes every possible effort to safeguard his wealth against illicit earnings, but there is always a possibility of some illicit earnings getting mixed up with that of his lawfully earned money or wealth. Take for example a clothes merchant. He sells a piece of cloth and receives payment unaware of the fact that the piece of cloth has developed holes in it and has become useless. Though he has been guilty of this mistake unknowingly, the money he has received is not legitimate for him and he has no right to own it. Even though he has received this money unknowingly, his body will not be blessed by the food bought and consumed, nor will his other assets be blessed in any way by the use of this money. But should such a person, in view of the divine commandment, spare a part of his wealth and donate it as Zakat, his wealth will continue to be purified. And even if there had been a part of his wealth which was not earned in a pure manner, it will return to its true owner, who is God, through Zakat rather than being spent on his personal comfort or pleasure. The remaining sum of his money will remain pure and clean, and everything that belongs to him will become blessed because of his consuming and benefitting from lawfully earned money.

The Life History of the Promised Messiah[as]

Another important thing which requires the attention of our Jamā'at is the preservation of the life history of the Promised Messiah[as]. By the grace of Allah, in this age, we have been provided with everything we need to accomplish this task; such as pen, ink, paper, printing press and the like. How sad would it be if we failed to act rightly in this regard? How will the people, who will follow us in time, view us? How would the people who are being converted to Aḥmadiyyat every day come to know about the person of the Promised Messiah[as] unless they have some means to undertake a detailed study of his life?

A few days back, two Christians visited here and had discussions with me. One of them asked another person: Was Mirza also like him? The answer the person gave to him was indeed very beautiful. He replied: 'Why do you ask me? Go and ask him about how the Promised Messiah[as] was and see what he has to say in this regard; but he calls himself a humble servant of Mirza and so you can infer for yourself what the Promised Messiah[as] must have been like.' So among the obligations that we hold most important, one is to preserve the biography and life history of the Promised Messiah[as] for future generations. It is very important for us to follow the ultimate example of excellence set by the Holy Prophet[sa], and then by his most true servant the Promised Messiah[as]. That is why it is highly important to set down the life history of the Promised Messiah[as]. Anyone who remembers some incident related to him should put it down and send that to me. We have been assigned this huge task, and we must accomplish it. I have already appointed a person to enquire from people and note down the experiences they had in this regard. The person has already started the job. Should someone amongst you recall any incident, he should put it in writing and send it to me so that all such incidents are compiled in one place and published, thereby getting preserved forever. There are still many among us, who have seen the Promised Messiah[as] and sat in his company, and who are able to narrate many incidents about him; but as the number of these people will decrease, it will become increasingly difficult to have sound knowledge about his life. Therefore, this task must be accomplished as soon as possible.

Other Important Issues

Settlement of Disputes

There is another important issue requiring your attention, namely that whenever you are faced with some matter which you think is controversial, or you have a difference of opinion among yourselves, you must not try to decide it on your own. Since, you have become united and part of the same fabric, you should refer such matters to us and get them decided. Send your mutual conflicts here. We shall seek help from God and decide the matter after properly investigating it.

Need for Primary Schools

One more thing to which I wish to draw your attention today is that it is essential for the intellectual development of the Jamā'at to open primary level schools in all places. Already, the work has started under my directive and by now some ten schools have been opened. All the Ahmadiyya Anjumans should try to open schools in their respective areas. Even if a school is already working in some area, an Ahmadiyya school is still needed, for in other schools the Holy Quran is not taught as a regular subject. That is why it has become imperative to open our own schools. Therefore, wherever possible, we should open our own schools. I have already appointed a sub-committee under Anjuman Taraqqi-e-Islam, which is responsible for making all arrangements required concerning opening such schools. All such arrangements can be made through correspondence with them.

Need for Preachers

Apart from these matters, our Jamā'at also needs preachers. They are particularly needed in large cities. Our cherished possession is the Holy Quran, and what else can be better than the Holy Quran? Therefore, I intend to initiate Darsul-Quran in various cities, and appoint at least one preacher in every district. But the number of those preachers who can really accomplish this task in our Jamā'at is small. Therefore, as you might be aware, a class of preachers has been initiated. Two students in this class delivered their lectures here yesterday. I have not yet been informed about what they said, but it is my wish that such people be fully prepared soon so that we can appoint them at some key places. In view of this, I have prepared a syllabus, and by studying it, the ten students of this class of preachers will be equipped with such knowledge as will make them fully capable of delivering Darsul-Quran within the next year. These students, I hope, will soon be able to do this job effectively and hopefully by December of next year they will be able to provide one preacher each to the communities at ten different places.

Learning the Meanings of the Holy Quran

I wish that all the members of our Jamā'at, men or women, know the Holy Quran very well. They should not only be able to read it, but they should also be well-versed in its meaning and translation. When one is unaware of the meanings of the Holy Quran, how can he truly appreciate its contents by repeated readings of the words alone? Until people are themselves able to translate the Holy Quran, we need an Urdu translation which should be free from the errors which are commonly found in the translations that are presently available.

Secondly, notes should be given on the verses which have been generally misunderstood so that misunderstandings can be removed and the supremacy of Islam is established over all other religions. Answers should be given to allegations raised against the Holy Quran and difficult points in it should be solved.

Every Ahmadi, male or female, must have a copy of the Holy Quran. Translation is already underway and the first part has been completed along with the notes. Should God so will, it will be published within a month. I wish it could be published part by part so that it could be made available to people without any delay. God Almighty says, 'We have revealed the Holy Quran gradually so that people could memorize it.' Similarly, we will also continue to publish it in parts so that people can read it easily and memorize it. A few of its manuscript copies have already arrived here. Translation of the second part is underway. Anjuman Taraqqi-e-Islam is publishing it. Every person should buy a separate copy for himself, his wife, and children.

Need for a Correspondence School

For the progress of the Jamā'at in religious knowledge, a distance learning school should be opened to impart education through correspondence. Some lessons should be prepared for those who are unable to stay in Qadian permanently to learn the Holy Quran.

These lessons should be sent to the students in parts. Once they have learned these parts, more assignments can then be sent. People should be able to raise the issues that arise in their minds by correspondence. In this way, while staying at home, they will be able to acquire some knowledge.

Tests for Knowledge of Books of the Promised Messiah[as]

The Promised Messiah[as] had an ardent desire that a course from his books is prepared and people should learn it and then take a test covering that syllabus during the *Jalsah Sālānah*. I sincerely desire that his wish should be fulfilled, and what he proposed should be implemented, so the examination should be held from next year onwards. Both parts of his book *Izāla-e-Auhām*, which relate to the non–Aḥmadīs, and *Surmah Chashm-e-Āryah*, which relates to the Āryas, should be studied and learned well. Any number of people should be allowed to take part in the competition. Those, whom God grants the life, should come for the *Jalsah* next year and those whom God enables to take the exam should sit the examination based on these books, so that their mistakes are corrected.

Settlement of Disagreements About the Doctrines

I also intend to address the doctrinal differences within the Jamā'at. I am trying to appoint some people to take care of all these matters, so that they should permanently record in writing, with references to the books of the Promised Messiah[as], the beliefs of the Ahmadiyya Jamā'at so that no such conflicts arise in future. How surprising is it that some thirty years after its inception, the Jamā'at is still faced with the debate on whether the Promised Messiah[as] was a Prophet or not. The reason for this is that those at the helm of this disagreement have failed to properly study the books of the Promised Messiah[as]; and if ever they had studied them, they did so with the preconceived belief that he was not a prophet. Their condition is the same as that of the Christians who study the Holy Quran from beginning to the end, yet they fail to find in it anything useful. In view of all this, I intend to appoint some people who should write a comprehensive booklet on this subject.

Other Needs of the Jamā'at

An important landmark of the time of the Promised Messiah[as] is the *Mināratul-Masīḥ*, about which he had said that once completed it would cause many blessings of Allah to descend. No appeal for financial contributions was made when its construction started. I had once said that it would itself attract contributions when we would start constructing it, in that people would on their own start making contributions. The Jamā'at in Qadian has volunteered around 500 rupees. I had not made any formal announcement; they arranged for this money on their own. The total sum of money that has been spent on the minaret so far is about 2000 rupees. Keeping this in mind, the members of the Jamā'at should try to contribute the remaining 1500 rupees.

Several other projects are underway. We ourselves have to make the financial sacrifices to carry them out. We have bid farewell to the non-Aḥmadīs; and some of those who initially belonged to us have now left us. So you are the only people left to pay attention to the other projects as well. There are a number of projects being completed under the auspices of Sadr Anjuman Ahmadiyya. They include two madrassahs, one high school and another school called the Ahmadiyya School. It is your children who will study at these schools. There is a guest house where guests stay and food is catered for them.

Besides this, there are a number of other things as well. The estimated expenses towards the propagation of Islam next year is around 24,000 rupees. The Holy Quran is being translated into English, and its publication is already underway. The proofs of *Sūrah al-Fātiḥah* have arrived. The translation of the first part of the Holy Quran has been completed. Financial contributions are required so that it can be published. There is also the propagation of Aḥmadiyyat in Britain. The expenses for this project are expected to be around six hundred rupees per month, since I wish to send one more missionary there. Tracts will also have to be published in English. Then there is an island near Africa called Mauritius where many English families are ready to embrace Islam. A missionary will be sent there as well. Correspondence in this regard is already underway.

Then there are the tracts which we publish. It has now been a few months since we last published a tract in Bengali. I am still receiving letters in which people are asking questions about it. Moreover, Sadr Anjuman Ahmadiyya has to pay off some debt, and it needs additional funds for future expenses. All these are the needs facing the Jamā'at today, and it is your obligation to meet these requirements. I hope you will not hesitate in making your best efforts in this regard. I now wish to read to you the point which the Holy Quran has made in regard to the service of one's faith. Almighty God says 'O Muslims! Never slack off on your work, and never be upset by the hardships that you may face in serving the faith. To quote:[12]

...اِنۡ تَکُوۡنُوۡا تَاۡلَمُوۡنَ فَاِنَّہُمۡ یَاۡلَمُوۡنَ کَمَا تَاۡلَمُوۡنَ ۚ وَ تَرۡجُوۡنَ مِنَ اللّٰہِ مَا لَا یَرۡجُوۡنَ ...

> If you suffer some pain or agony, the disbelievers suffer in the same way, but you hope to receive rewards from Allah which they cannot hope for.

Therefore, you should also remember that though you might feel burdened on account of these repeated requests for making financial contributions, keep in mind that the enemies of Islam are laying down their lives and spending their wealth too in order to destroy Islam. In terms of hardships there is no difference between you and them, but the rewards which you are hoping to receive cannot be attained by them. Therefore, how painful would it be if, in spite of all these good expectations, you still show slackness; whereas the enemies, in spite of being smitten with every kind of hopelessness, should continue their work and face every kind of hardship for the sake of spreading mere falsehood?

The door to divine rewards is open to you. You should seek to attain this reward as much as you can. At the moment, we are in need of money, but God is Self-Sufficient. He needs no help from anyone. In fact, He has provided our Jamā'at with this opportunity to serve the faith. He has done this as His sheer grace towards us; otherwise, His enterprise is such that it can never suffer. Some

---

[12] *Sūrah an-Nisā'*, 4:105

people have left us, but our work is continuing. The one who serves God, enters the fold of His helpers. So continue to do your work to the best of your ability. Last year, the Jamā'at in District Gurdaspur contributed six or seven thousand rupees. Hopefully, this year too, God willing, they will contribute two or three thousand more than the previous year. This is aside from what they contribute regularly every month. For the rest of the amount needed, the effort is to be made by you all. May Allah enable you to fulfil the task for which He has founded the Ahmadiyya Jamā'at.

SECOND SPEECH:
OBJECTS OF HUMAN LIFE

(December 28, 1914)

بِسۡمِ اللّٰہِ الرَّحۡمٰنِ الرَّحِیۡمِ
نَحۡمَدُہٗ وَ نُصَلِّیۡ عَلٰی رَسُوۡلِہِ الۡکَرِیۡمِ [1]

After reciting *tashahhud, ta'awwudh*, and *Sūrah al-Fātiḥah*, Ḥuḍūr[ra] recited the following verses of the Holy Quran:[2]

اَللّٰہُ لَاۤ اِلٰہَ اِلَّا ہُوَ ۚ اَلۡحَیُّ الۡقَیُّوۡمُ ۬ۚ لَا تَاۡخُذُہٗ سِنَۃٌ وَّ لَا نَوۡمٌ ؕ لَہٗ مَا فِی السَّمٰوٰتِ
وَ مَا فِی الۡاَرۡضِ ؕ مَنۡ ذَا الَّذِیۡ یَشۡفَعُ عِنۡدَہٗۤ اِلَّا بِاِذۡنِہٖ ؕ یَعۡلَمُ مَا بَیۡنَ اَیۡدِیۡہِمۡ وَ مَا
خَلۡفَہُمۡ ۚ وَ لَا یُحِیۡطُوۡنَ بِشَیۡءٍ مِّنۡ عِلۡمِہٖۤ اِلَّا بِمَا شَآءَ ۚ وَسِعَ کُرۡسِیُّہُ السَّمٰوٰتِ
وَ الۡاَرۡضَ ۚ وَ لَا یَـُٔوۡدُہٗ حِفۡظُہُمَا ۚ وَ ہُوَ الۡعَلِیُّ الۡعَظِیۡمُ ﴿۲۵۶﴾

---

1 In the name of Allah, the Gracious, the Merciful; we praise Him and invoke blessings upon His Noble Messenger.

2 Allah—there is no God but He, the Living, the Self-Subsisting and All-Sustaining. Slumber seizes Him not, nor sleep. To Him belongs whatsoever is in the heavens and whatsoever is in the earth. Who is he that will intercede with Him except by His permission? He knows what is before them and what is behind them; and they encompass nothing of His knowledge except what He pleases. His throne extends over the heavens and the earth; and the care of them burdens Him not; and He is the High, the Great. (*Sūrah al-Baqarah*, 2:256)

Ḥuḍūr[ra] said:

Yesterday, I said that I wished to speak on a subject which is of so much importance that I cannot find words to fully expound its need and grandeur.

Importance of the Subject

The object of every man's life is but one. There only is one way that any sect, nation, or Jamā'at can prosper; and there is only one thing which can prove mankind to indeed be worthy of being called human beings. Should God enable me, I now wish to speak to you on that one point.

By the grace of Allah, yesterday, though I spoke for about three and a half hours, I suffered no complications. But because of speaking yesterday, I am not feeling well today. That is why I will not be able to give as detailed an elaboration of this subject today, but should God enable me to do so, I will speak on it another time.

Some of you might be wondering what it is that is so important that a Jamā'at cannot progress without it, or that man cannot truly become man without it, or the very purpose of human life will be left incomplete without it. Then again, if it is such an important point why was it not explained by the Promised Messiah[as] or by Ḥaḍrat Khalīfatul-Masīḥ I[ra]? I must point out that the importance of something is not diminished by hearing it repeatedly. I have not come up with an idea that was not known to the world before. It is the same thing that you have heard many times before my exposition to you, but until it is fully acted upon and becomes well-established, the need for re-iterating it will continue.

Behold, quinine is very effective in treating malaria and is given to hundreds of patients suffering from malaria daily, and so as long as malaria exists in the world, the need for quinine will also continue to exist. Similarly, water is essential for the existence of every living being. Should someone ask what is indispensable for life, and then get the response that water is one of them—and upon hearing this says that since this is something we drink daily, why consider it so important—he will be utterly wrong, because as long as life is dependent upon water, water will continue to be important. Even if someone drinks it many times a day, the need for it is beyond any doubt. We do not have to pay anything for air. It is automatically inhaled through the process of respiration and this has always been the case, yet its need and significance will never diminish. It is as useful and important today as it was at any time in the past.

Therefore, though you have already heard what I am going to say today, until it fully establishes itself in the world and all people start acting upon it, I will continue to speak of it and its importance shall never fade. I now come to the point. Some people should note it down so that it is recorded for those who have not been able to come here today so that they can also derive benefit from it. But I want to re-emphasize that you must not underestimate its value. It is indeed a thing of great import. The fact that many people fail to understand the real importance of something truly significant often results in their ruin, thereby causing them to suffer complete devastation. Wise is he who gives due consideration to everything, contemplates their consequences and ponders over their reality. Let me explain this point with a parable.

There was a man. He once said to his nephews. 'Tomorrow after the meal, I will bring you a *laddū*[3] to eat. It has been prepared by hundreds of thousands of people.' They were surprised to hear that and thought that the *laddū* that has been prepared by a hundred thousand of people, must be of gigantic proportions. The next day when they sat to eat, neither of them would take more than a couple of spoonfuls lest they filled their stomachs with various foods and be deprived of the true taste of that *laddū*. When they had finished eating the meal, the nephews reminded their uncle of his promise of bringing for them a *laddū* made by a hundred thousand people. They requested him to fulfil his promise. He said that he certainly remembered his promise and having said that put before them a *laddū* like the ones commonly sold in the market. The boys were disappointed when they saw the *laddū* and said, 'You had promised that you would bring a *laddū* made by almost a hundred thousand people, but now you have put before us an ordinary *laddū*. What is the meaning of this?' Their uncle said, 'Go and bring a pen and start making the list of people who took part in the making of this *laddū*, and then I shall prove that this *laddū* has indeed been made by several hundred thousand people. Observe that a sweets merchant has made it, but the things that have been used to make it were bought by the sweets merchant from different people. Every thing from among those things was then made by thousand of men. Take sugar for instance. How many thousands

[3] An Indian confection, typically made from flour, sugar, and shortening, that is shaped into a ball.

have done the hard work of making it? There are those whose job was only to mix its ingredients. Then there were those who extracted its juice from the sugarcane after harvesting the crop. Then there are those who ploughed the fields and watered them. There were those who had mined, refined and made it into iron blades; and those who had cut down the trees to get and shape the wood used in the tillers. In short, if I count all these people, how far will their number go? Then imagine the number of those who made the flour used in it. Similarly, if you count the people who have made all these things, does their number not then reach millions? Having heard this, the nephews confessed that he was right. Therefore, you should also remember it very well that a thing's significance is not contingent upon its amount and quantity. Rather, it depends upon its eventual outcome and ultimate benefit, and so what I am going to set forth now is very important. No one should underestimate its value and get disappointed like young children who hastily declare it to be a simple thing, even though it does apparently seem to be minor. The fact is that it is indeed a matter of great import. Should you learn it and act upon it, God has promised that He will make such person honoured in both here in this world and in the hereafter. I firmly believe this promise to be true, and declare in the name of God that if your actions are in accordance with the guidance I am about to give, you will certainly be the recipients of the promised blessings.

Attaining Nearness to Allah

People ask how they can attain nearness to God. Remember it well that if you will act according to what I say, you will attain divine nearness not only in the hereafter, but in this very world. God shall speak to you not only after your death, but He will also speak to you in this very world. So reflect upon it carefully. I know, and it is customary among audiences, that after they happen to hear a good lecture, they say that it was very enjoyable or the speech was excellent, and so on. They are not able to realize the pain with which the speaker addresses them. The result of listening to the lecture should be quite different. The speaker speaks with a heart-felt agony, but those who listen evade the issue by saying that the speech was enjoyable. You have not come here to enjoy yourselves, nor have you come to attend some comical performances. Someone who has made this journey for this purpose shall be held answerable before God for the money that he spent on this journey. Therefore, you should listen to every lecture with due attention and open ears, and bear it well in mind and rather act upon it.

I have always wished that God would enable me, even on my deathbed, to make it the last thing I say; and should I have to re-start by saying something, the same should be the first thing that I say. All worldly things as compared to it are worthless. The worldly gains and material advantages are all useless, and the means for self-indulgence and luxury are of no avail.

It has become a big problem nowadays that people think in terms of how enjoyable a lecture is. But O my dears! Having spent your money you have not come here for the purpose of enjoyment or extravaganza; rather, your purpose coming here, and my purpose of calling you here is quite different. If someone fails to understand this purpose, he surely has not come for us, but has come here to please his own self. He, who has come here merely for some enjoyment or for amusing himself with some extravaganza, has indeed committed a sin. If someone ever had such a thought, he must repent and seek forgiveness from Allah. A person, who wastes his money and time and leaves his homeland and dear ones only for the sake of amusing himself, will surely be held accountable before God for every single penny and moment that he spends as to why he laid Allah's bounty to waste. Therefore, ponder over it sincerely and bring about a transformation in yourselves. Do not listen to the lecture for the sake of amusement only.

All kinds of things are said in the lectures. Some are meant to be amusing also, but you should never wish that a lecture should only contain amusing things and that you will pay attention only to those things. Do not look for comedy or tragedy in a lecture; rather, pay attention to what the lecturer says. Should you feel uncomfortable at any point, reflect upon it; and should you like some point, react to it by acting upon it. Do not sit in a lecture only for listening to entertaining stories.

There is another problem with those who listen to these lectures, and that is that every listener thinks of himself as pure of all ills, and that the lecture is meant for those sitting around him. As a consequence all of them leave the lecture empty-handed, and the lecture does not avail anything to anybody. Hence, every one of you should think that you are the first person to whom I am addressing this lecture and should think that whatever has been said has been said for you alone. Should there be a saint in the audience, my address is meant for him; and should there be a person with the most base and impure morals, I am speaking to him as well. Those who think that an address is not meant for them, rather is meant for others, deprive only themselves.

It is narrated that, in order to test his courtiers' loyalty, a king ordered everyone of them to pour a receptacle of water into a specific pond. When they left for their homes, all of them wondered why they should burden themselves with carrying a receptacle of water and pouring it into the pond. How could those ministers and elite for whom it was difficult to even lift a fallen handkerchief carry a receptacle of water! Every one of them thought that the pouring of merely one receptacle of water by him was not going to fill the pond anyway. Thousands will pour their receptacles. The king would never come to know whether someone poured his due or not, and so every one of them, having thought the same thing, failed to pour the water. Therefore the pond remained dry. When the king arrived to inspect it, he found the pond to be completely dry. He reproached all the courtiers telling them to have shame and asking them if this was the way to execute an order. But instead of being ashamed and regretful, everyone started reproaching the others: 'Why didn't you pour your receptacle? I thought everyone would pour his, so it should cause no harm if I failed to pour mine. Your slackness has resulted in my disgrace.' Thus, every one of them tried to lay the blame for his own laziness and inefficiency upon the others.

Therefore, if all the listeners of lectures think that the address is not meant for them and someone else is being addressed, the consequence will be that all will remain ignorant as ever. But if everyone should think that whatever has been said is meant for him and that it is incumbent upon him to act upon it, all will benefit from it. Despite this, if there is someone who fails to understand something, God shall cover his faults in view of the tiding conveyed in:

لا يشقى جليسهم

[Saying of the Holy Prophet that no one attending a righteous company will be deprived of its blessings]. Due to the others being righteous and God-fearing the faults of those who are not so fortunate are also covered up. For instance, if the King's courtiers had poured their receptacles and a few had failed to do so, their default would have remained concealed. In short, whatever is said is meant for everyone, from the eldest to the youngest. No one should consider that others are the only ones being addressed. Only then can all of us truly benefit.

Turn to Allah

I now set forth what I invite you to, and what the important point is to which I have drawn your attention. Listen! It is just one word, and no more, and that is 'Allah'. I call upon you to turn to Him alone. All that I voice is for His sake alone. To call towards Him do I sound this bugle. Hence, he whom God enables and guides should come to me and respond to my call.

There are many things in the world which are very beautiful and pleasing to the eyes; but however beautiful a thing is, it has been created by God. It is God who has bestowed upon it such beauty and attractiveness. That is why there is nothing which can be on par with God's beauty and excellence. But despite the fact that God is the most beautiful and the most lovable of all, the most Benevolent and Beneficent of all, the world—incapable world—looks at Him with contempt and disdain. He is the Lord of all the worlds, and before His glory and grandeur everything lies worthless, but the way He is being treated by the world is utterly deplorable.

Ḥaḍrat Khalīfatul-Masīḥ I[ra] used to relate about one of his teachers that he saw a dream when he was in Bhopal that he was standing near a bridge in the outskirts of the town. There he found a leper whose whole body had been infested with worms. The flies were resting on his body. He asked him who he was. He said that he was God, his Lord. He said that he had read so much praiseworthy about God in the Holy Quran; that He is so beautiful and there is none who is comparable to Him. What has become of His condition? God replied to him, 'My countenance that you are seeing is not the one I possess in reality. This is how I look through the eyes of the people of Bhopal.'

Examine yourselves closely, and analyze your actions, your words, your sayings; the time you are moving and the moments you are resting. How you see God as compared to the things that you love in this world, lest your view of God be the same as, or similar to, the people of Bhopal. Remember it well that God is entirely free and pure of all ugliness, vice and disfigurement.

Story of Ḥaḍrat Ādam[as]

It is sad to see how some Muslims react to the story of Ḥaḍrat Adam in the Holy Quran. Some Muslims ask why, on the instigation of the Satan, Ḥaḍrat Ādam[as] caused us to be expelled from the paradise for the sake of a grain of wheat. They say if it were them [instead of Ḥaḍrat Ādam[as]], they would not have been expelled. They ignore the fact that Satan caused not only Ḥaḍrat Ādam[as] to be expelled from heaven, but is also trying to throw them out. They lament that Ḥaḍrat Ādam[as] was charmed and deceived once by Satan, but they forget that they are themselves being deceived by him every day and are always accompanied by him. They try to find reasons why Ḥaḍrat Ādam[as] was deceived, but they do not know that Satan is always sitting by them and inciting them for evil. Instead of expressing discontent and speaking ill of Ḥaḍrat Ādam[as], they should lament their own selves. How could Ḥaḍrat Ādam[as] expel people from the paradise? Everyone is expelled from the paradise on account of his own sins. No one is expelled due to anything that Ādam[as] did.

The Christians believe that they inherited sin from Ḥaḍrat Ādam[as], and for that reason they were expelled from paradise. But God in the Holy Quran categorically states:[4]

لَقَدْ خَلَقْنَا الْإِنْسَانَ فِيْٓ اَحْسَنِ تَقْوِيْمٍ ۝

Surely, We have created man in the best make.

The question now is if God had created man in the best make, how can He expel anyone from paradise as a punishment for the sin committed by someone else? Every child that is born in the world has his abode in the paradise. But then he destroys that home with his own hands and builds a home in hell. Therefore, you must never think that it was some other Ādam that was expelled from heaven;

---

4 *Sūrah at-Tīn*, 95:5

rather, it is you who are constantly chased by the Satan which ultimately causes many to be expelled from heaven. Whether someone has been captivated by Satan already or not, in both cases one has to remain vigilant to secure himself. Suppose that someone tells a group of people sitting together that one of them would be hanged. Now if everyone of them were to keep sitting and assume that someone else, and not he, would be hanged, one of them will surely lose his life. But should all of them leave that place, they will all be saved, for who could have predicted which one of them was going to be hanged?

Beauty and Grandeur of Allah and His Kingdom

I emphasize that people have become careless in their relationship with God. The fact is that there is none more beautiful, more loving, and more enchanting than Him. Should you love someone, love Him. Should you have a beloved, He is the one. Should there be anyone to fear, it is He. Should you feel awed by someone, feel awed by Him. If you attain Him, you are no longer in need of anyone else, and no hindrance will be able to obstruct your way. Therefore, let yourselves melt at His threshold and transform yourselves. What God is and how beautiful He is can be read about in *Sūrah al-Fātiḥah*. Should you see just one flash of His beauty, you will no longer stand in need of beholding any other beauty. Man is enamoured and charmed by the beauty of worldly things, but what he should do is to reflect upon the beauty of the Creator who has brought the beautiful things into existence. To see God, one is not required to see outward; the beauty of God is obvious to the heart of every person. Anyone who honestly reflects can reach Him very quickly. Every single iota of all that exists in the world is testifying to the existence of God Almighty. There is nothing in the world which does not vociferously proclaim the evidence in favour of the existence of a God who is the Creator of both space and time. The piece of paper you are holding, the pen, the table and chair, the very earth you are sitting on, the clothes that you are wearing, your hands, feet, nose and ears; everything provides evidence that God does, in fact, exist. People like fine clothing, beautiful women, delicious food and plenty of wealth. Reflect then as to how beautiful is the one who has created them! So why don't you fall in love with Him? [Allah the Almighty says in the Holy Quran]:[5]

اَللّٰهُ لَآ اِلٰهَ اِلَّا هُوَ ۚ اَلْحَيُّ الْقَيُّوْمُ ۚ لَا تَاْخُذُهٗ سِنَةٌ وَّلَا نَوْمٌ ؕ لَهٗ مَا فِي السَّمٰوٰتِ
وَمَا فِي الْاَرْضِ ؕ مَنْ ذَا الَّذِيْ يَشْفَعُ عِنْدَهٗٓ اِلَّا بِاِذْنِهٖ ؕ يَعْلَمُ مَا بَيْنَ اَيْدِيْهِمْ وَمَا
خَلْفَهُمْ ۚ وَلَا يُحِيْطُوْنَ بِشَيْءٍ مِّنْ عِلْمِهٖٓ اِلَّا بِمَا شَآءَ ۚ وَسِعَ كُرْسِيُّهُ السَّمٰوٰتِ
وَالْاَرْضَ ۚ وَلَا يَـُٔوْدُهٗ حِفْظُهُمَا ۚ وَهُوَ الْعَلِيُّ الْعَظِيْمُ ﴿٢٥٦﴾

---

[5] Allah—there is no God but He, the Living, the Self-Subsisting and All-Sustaining. Slumber seizes Him not, nor sleep. To Him belongs whatsoever is in the heavens and whatsoever is in the earth. Who is he that will intercede with Him except by His permission? He knows what is before them and what is behind them; and they encompass nothing of His knowledge except what He pleases. His throne extends over the heavens and the earth; and the care of them burdens Him not; and He is the High, the Great. (*Sūrah al-Baqarah*, 2:256)

These verses are indeed magnificent, and impart a glorious teaching. It was customary on the part of the Holy Prophet[sa] to recite these verses three times and blow over his body every night before going to bed. It is incumbent upon every Muslim to follow his Sunnah. The first thing to which man has been called upon in these verses is:[6]

اَللّٰہُ لَآ اِلٰہَ اِلَّا ھُوَ ...

That is, behold O man that there is none who is worthy of your worship except God.

In the world, things are valued depending upon their scarcity. Take water for example. Although is an essential commodity, people do not try to save it. The reason is that they know that they will get it whenever they need it. Air is essential for life but no one tries to save it; everyone knows that whenever it is required, it will automatically be inhaled by the body through its normal channels. But the same water that is generally not valued becomes extremely valuable in a desert where water is scares. At such a time, if someone possesses a glass of water and is asked to sell it for millions of rupees, he will refuse to do so. We only come to know the value of a thing depending upon the need it assumes. Grains, when found in large quantities, are available at cheap rates, but they become expensive when they are scarce. Similarly, if there had been several gods, it might have caused people to say that should they fail to attain to one of them, they would always have the chance to attain to another one, but:[7]

---

6 *Ibid.*

7 *Ibid.*

اَللّٰهُ لَآ اِلٰهَ اِلَّا هُوَ ...

Allah—there is no God but He...

Should someone imagine that he will find another god besides Him, he would find it impossible, because, God is one—not two, nor three, nor four, nor thousands or millions. Since there is only one God, where else can one go after leaving Him? You need Him all the time, and at every moment you require His help. People do at times annoy worldly kings, for they can always leave for another country. One can go to Iran if the king in China happens to be cruel; or one can take refuge in England if he is victimized by the kingdom of Iran. But where can one go to flee from God? There is no land that is not possessed by Him, and no kingdom which is not fully under His control. Man has no other God to seek help from. Hindus believe there are many gods, and that these gods also have quarrels amongst themselves. It is recorded [in their books] that Shiva was angry with someone and killed him, but the deceased was a beloved of Brahma. So, Brahma said, 'It is I who create, and I will revive him,' and so Brahma brought him back to life. Shiva kept killing him and Brahma kept reviving him. Hence, their conflict continued.

These are thoughts shared only by Hindus. We do not have any such gods that if one should kill someone, another would restore him to life and should one be angry, another would comfort him. A servant can deny serving his master, for he can find employment somewhere else. But we can never behave in this way towards God. He alone is our Master. We have no other Master besides Him.[8]

---

[8] ... the Living, the Self-Subsisting and All-Sustaining. *Ibid.*

...اَلْحَیُّ الْقَیُّوْمُ ...

The worldly masters who are all mortal, but the Master we believe in never suffers death. He is eternal, and He is not someone from whom we can ever break away. He is also Self-Subsisting. Can one excuse himself by saying that he had previously served a different master, and so he owes his due respect to him as well? Our God says that He is not only our God now, but He is the Lord that has existed from time immemorial, and so we are not indebted to any one besides Him. He is the God who is Everlasting and through whom everything else exists. So, we are indebted to none else but Him. The word قَیُّوْمُ has two connotations: firstly, Self-subsisting; secondly, Causing others to subsist.[9]

...لَا تَاْخُذُهٗ سِنَةٌ وَّلَا نَوْمٌ ...

One may say that though he accepts that God is one, is without associate and is eternal and that He has been our Lord in the past as well as the present; but there is a possibility that he is overpowered by slumber and falls asleep and then His courtiers replace Him and take up His business, so we should also try to cultivate good relations with them and try to please them. Almighty God has made it clear here that your Lord is in fact the one who never slumbers nor falls asleep. You must not consider Him like the worldly kings and sovereigns whose courtiers have to be flattered before you can see the kings themselves. Your Lord is not the one who can suffer any slumber or sleep. He is eternally awake, and stands guard over

---

9 ... slumber seizes Him not, nor sleep... *Ibid.*

everything. What a fine point of divine wisdom is contained in the verse:[10]

...لَا تَأْخُذُهُۥ سِنَةٌ وَلَا نَوْمٌ...

... Slumber seizes Him not, nor sleep...

In elegant composition the order in which the minor and major points are arranged is a key to eloquence and elegance of expression. For instance, we can say that a person is not seriously ill, and as a matter of fact, he is not ill at all. But if we say that a person is not suffering a minor illness, and that he is not seriously ill either, such a construction would be obviously wrong. This is the reason why major things are mentioned first and minor things later. And here God makes a point by saying that He neither suffers slumber nor does He fall asleep. In denying slumber, His falling deep asleep has already been denied. So what was the reason that He also had to deny falling asleep? Remember that the words of God are never without wisdom. There is a point of deep wisdom in it, namely, that سِنَةٌ denotes the time when one's eyes close involuntarily because one is totally overpowered by sleep. One slumbers when feeling very sleepy, and does not slumber until he is completely overwhelmed by sleep. So here God has clearly denied that His work can ever cause Him any tiredness, which would cause Him to suffer even the slightest episode of slumber; nor can He ever feel so

---

[10] *Ibid.*

overwhelmed by sleep that it should cause His eyes to doze off. Moreover, He is also not in need of ordinary sleep.[11]

...لَهٗ مَا فِي السَّمٰوٰتِ وَمَا فِي الْاَرْضِ ؕ مَنْ ذَا الَّذِيْ يَشْفَعُ عِنْدَهٗۤ اِلَّا بِاِذْنِهٖ ؕ...

God asks man while His Lord is the possessor of all that is in the heavens and the earth, how can man then take someone else as his Lord? There are people who say that they do not worship anyone beside Allah. They add that [by visiting and prostrating at the graves] they only mean to pay their respects and make their offerings, because they, being the beloved of God, would intercede on our behalf leading to the fulfilment of our hearts' desires. But God says that there is none who can intercede with Him without His permission.

In this age, who was more pious than the Promised Messiah[as]? But once when he prayed for the recovery of Nawwāb Abdur-Rahim[ra], the son of Nawwāb Muhammad Ali Khan[ra], from his illness, he received a revelation to the effect that he was not going to survive. The Promised Messiah[as] felt deeply concerned by this thought, because Nawwāb Muhammad Ali Khan[ra] was planning to move to Qadian leaving all his assets behind, and should his son depart from the world he might undergo a trial. That is why he supplicated to God, 'O my Allah! I intercede for the health of this boy'. Thereupon, the Promised Messiah[as] received the revelation:

---

11 To Him belongs whatsoever is in the heavens and whatsoever is in the earth. Who is he that will intercede with Him except by His permission? *Ibid.*

مَنْ ذَا الَّذِیْ یَشْفَعُ عِنْدَہٗۤ اِلَّا بِاِذْنِہٖ

Who is it that will intercede with Him except by His permission? (*Tadhkirah*, second English Edition p. 643, published by Islam International Publications, 2009)

Behold! How glorious was the status of the Promised Messiah[as]. His advent was being awaited by the whole world for thirteen hundred years. But even he, when trying to interceding without permission, was thus warned by God, ' who are you to intercede without first asking My permission?' The Promised Messiah[as] has written that when he received this revelation, he fell down and started trembling. He felt as if he was on the verge of dying, but having seen him in this condition, God thus spoke to him: All right. I permit you to intercede. Go ahead. So through his intercession, Abdur-Rahim Khan recovered, and is still alive by the grace of Allah. The Promised Messiah[as] was able to do this merely by the grace of God, and so if God does not allow that even a person like the Promised Messiah[as] should intercede without His permission, where do those stand who have been ascribed loftiness by people. They simply have no standing, and therefore can never intercede. We learn from the *aḥādīth* that on the Day of Judgment the Holy Prophet[sa] will be given permission by God to intercede and he will intercede after the permission is granted. In the presence of all this evidence, how ignorant is the person who considers someone to be able to intercede for him.[12]

یَعْلَمُ مَا بَیْنَ اَیْدِیْھِمْ وَمَا خَلْفَھُمْ ۚ

[12] He knows what is before them and what is behind them. *Ibid.*

Then there is another thing to be discussed. One may accept that one cannot really intercede without being permitted from God, but just as kings have courtiers through whom one can comfortably have access to the king, God must also have some courtiers. God states that these fools do not even know why kings have courtiers. They have them because the kings are always in need of getting the latest information through them, for, on their own, they cannot know what is going on in the country. For instance, how can our king come to know what is happening in India while he is sitting in England? It is for this purpose that he has appointed the viceroy. But how can even a viceroy come to know what is happening all over India—in the north and south, east and west? And so for this purpose lieutenant governors have been appointed. Again, how can the lieutenant governors find out on their own what is going on in the whole province? For this purpose deputy commissioners have been appointed. To keep these deputy commissioners well-informed, a number of other people such as Tehsildars, Assistant Tehsildars, and Lumbardars, Patwaries, and watchmen have been appointed. It is in this way that all the news and secrets get to the kings. Otherwise, they can never come to know of the situation on their own. As for God, He Himself states that He knows all about your past and future. Then why should He consider Himself in need of any courtiers? يَعْلَمُ مَا بَيْنَ اَيْدِيْهِمْ وَمَا خَلْفَهُمْ ۚ connotes two things:

1. God knows that which is yet to happen, and also that which you have done in the past.
2. He knows all the actions that you have taken, and also the good deeds that you should have done, but failed to do.

So when He is All-Aware, why would He feel the need for any courtiers?[13]

...وَلَا يُحِيطُونَ بِشَيْءٍ مِّنْ عِلْمِهِۦٓ إِلَّا بِمَا شَآءَ...

Moreover, how can one reach the depths of His knowledge? No one can ever come to know of the true nature of His being through one's own efforts, only those come to know of it whom He Himself grants cognition. Even then, one only knows of Him to the extent that He wills.[14]

...وَسِعَ كُرْسِيُّهُ ٱلسَّمَٰوَٰتِ وَٱلْأَرْضَ...

His knowledge encompasses both the heavens and earth.

Again:[15]

...وَلَا يَـُٔودُهُۥ حِفْظُهُمَا...

One may put forth the idea that though God has not appointed any courtiers to remain well-informed about things; but He must have appointed some assistants in order to help him conduct His job, for we see that the worldly rulers have armies and police for protection and for running the affairs of the state. God states that He does not require these things either. He is managing everything on His own

---

13 *Ibid.*

14 *Ibid.*

15 ...and the care of them burdens Him not. *Ibid.*

and His power is such that He controls everything and there is nothing that can cause him to get tired.[16]

...وَهُوَ الْعَلِيُّ الْعَظِيْمُ ۝

There is now only one possible objection left, namely, that even if we agree that God does not need anybody's help in order to keep Himself well-informed, He must have appointed some courtiers to display His might and glory. God has rejected this notion by saying وَهُوَ الْعَلِيُّ الْعَظِيْمُ that is, He is the Greatest; there is nothing which can make Him greater by its help and support. Whatever stands by Him, stands for an elevation in its own stature and not for that of God. Therefore, it is absolutely wrong to think that God might have employed courtiers for the sake of demonstrating His might and glory. God prevails over everything. There is nothing that can refuse to submit to Him.

Such is our God—the True God. There is none who is like Him. How unfortunate it would be if, having such a Lord, one should still look for someone else! If a person is provided excellent food, but he wants to consume filth; or if he is provided excellent clothing, but prefers to wrap a dirty rag around him, can such a person deserve to be called wise and sane? Definitely not! Wise is he who opts for what is better. Hence, know for sure that there is none who is better than God. I wish to impress upon you that you should always keep God and His pleasure in view, for all that exists in the world is nothing as compared with Him, and there is nothing that can stand equal to Him. You find the moon shining and pleasing to eyes, yet can anyone call this to be an inherent characteristic of the

---

[16] ...and He is the High, the Great. *Ibid.*

moon? Not at all! The moon takes proper pride for reflecting the light of the sun. But again, is the sun shining because it is personally possessed of some light? No. Rather, the fact is that it gets its light from the Gracious God. Therefore, if the moon is shining and the sun is bright, and we consider them both to be useful and beautiful to look at, then their beauty and usefulness are drawing our attention to the beauty of God and the magnificent attributes possessed by Him, such as His graciousness and nobility.

Everything of beauty found in the world that we call beautiful, has been bestowed its beauty by God. That is why He alone is the one who is possessed of every beauty. God has thus stated in *Sūrah al-Fātiḥah* اَلْحَمْدُ لِلّٰهِ رَبِّ الْعٰلَمِيْنَ, or that, All praise belongs to Allah and to none else, for He alone is the Lord of all the worlds. He is the Creator of all that exists, and He alone is their Provider. Since He provides for everything, why should all the praise not belong to Him? Parents raise their children and provide for them, but do you know who has imbued their hearts with love for their child? It is God who has caused this to happen. When someone gives away a penny to a beggar, we say he has done a commendable act. But the fact is that his heart was inspired by God to do so. Similarly, every good act done by someone is attributed to God. That is why all praise really belongs to God and to no one else. For instance, if a master tells his servant to distribute some money among the beggars, the master will deserve the praise though the distribution will be done by the servant. Similarly, when a man does a good deed, he does it on behalf of his Lord like the distribution of the wealth of a master, for there is nothing which the man possesses as a personal right; rather, everything belongs to God.

Therefore, all the benevolence, good manners, beauty and charming attributes that anyone has, belong to God; for the entire world is in His service, and there is no other master beside Him. People face a lot of hardships due to their parents, wives, children, wealth, kinsman and other close relations in matters of faith. But one has to remember that God is God and humans are humans. Whenever faced with some problem, you must reflect upon what pleases God; and when you have realized what God's will is, work towards attaining His pleasure no matter what sacrifice you have to make.

No Associate with God

To take this matter one step further, I will say that a man must not hold any associate with God. God is one. I believe no Ahmadi is a disbeliever of His Unity. God has enabled them to truly believe in His Oneness. That is why I am sure that no Ahmadi will ever prostrate before false gods or try to attach himself to anyone beside God. The rest of the world has relinquished faith, but you are the Jamā'at that has given their word that they will always keep their faith above all worldly considerations. God has therefore promised to this Jamā'at that He will cause it to flourish. This indeed is the Jamā'at of the elect of God. Therefore, one cannot really presume that this Jamā'at will ever get involved in manifest idol worship.

I wish to make you aware that much of religion has turned to worldly rituals. But such practice of religion can never bring one close to God; not even to the slightest degree. I call you to follow the religion so that with each step one should get closer to God. Should you move towards Him, your prayers and supplications will be granted acceptance a thousand times more than they are accepted now and you will be shown the blessed results of your good deeds with your own eyes. By the grace of Allah, you are treading upon the right path, but still you have to be extremely cautious and vigilant. Satan is wont to mislead you at times on the plea of the world, and at times on the plea of the faith. Therefore, what I want to explain to you is that whatever worship you offer, perform it with the intent of pleasing God alone. There should be no other motive in your mind.

At the time of every prayer, you must delve deep into your hearts and see whether you are offering it to win the pleasure of God or you have some other intent hidden at the back of your mind. When it comes to making financial contributions, look deep into your soul to reflect whether you gave it for the sake of winning divine pleasure, or did you give it away just because someone came to your door and asked for it. Those who collect these contributions do not really know your intent, but you know your intent very well. You must always bear in mind that you make these contributions for the sake of the faith and to please God. Likewise, you must have God in mind in everything that you do. When you will make this your guiding principle and intent, the worship you perform will bear better fruit. With every passing moment, and with every passing day, you will continue to flourish and prosper.

Behold! The result of an action varies depending upon the intention behind it. Having seen a wasp or scorpion sitting on someone's body, one knows that it would definitely sting the person, if it is not removed. That is why, one may removes it by slamming it with some force. This causes the one who is hit to be thankful and appreciative of his action. But should someone do it with the intent of hurting someone, he will surely be punished. Hence, a change in the intent can make the same action produce two different results. Therefore, worship and virtuous deeds should not be done just because you are used to them. Rather, you should do them with solemn intention behind them.

Many people ask for money in the name of the nation. They say do this and do that for the nation, but I ask, what is the value of the nation? You should not make financial contributions for the sake of your nation; rather, you should make financial sacrifices for the sake of God Almighty. Refrain from ever uttering such sinful words. Have their existed no nations before you? Were you without any relatives in the past? If they existed, then why was this new Jamā'at needed? Remember it well that what you call a nation has no value at all [in comparison with God.] God alone is the One to consider. Therefore, all your actions should be directed towards God and for His sake alone. Submit yourself to Him while walking, moving around, sleeping or in wakefulness. Should you do this, your actions will certainly become ever more fruitful.

Perform Good Deeds with Noble Intentions

There are many people who do things out of habit without realizing why they are doing them. They do it because they are accustomed to doing it, and derive no benefit whatsoever. Just consider a Muslim who does not use his left hand to eat, but instead uses his right one. Do you know the reason for doing so? The reason is that the Holy Prophet Muhammad[sa] has commanded him to eat with his right hand. But I ask, how many times have you reflected that you are doing this due to a commandment given by the Holy Prophet[sa]? Just have a look at the last three or four years of your life and see how many times you have thought so. There are so many among the Muslims who may have never considered the reasons why they eat with their right hand, and not their left. Indeed, it is virtuous to eat with one's right hand, for one who does so, acts in accordance with the commandment of the Holy Prophet[sa]. But how can a person who eats with his right hand out of habit, and not because the Holy Prophet[sa] has commanded him to do so, deserve any reward? He certainly deserves no reward, whatsoever. Young children, when they feel like passing water, put themselves in a position on the bed akin to that of the prostration during the prayer. However, does this act of theirs make them deserving of any reward? Never!

There are many things which are done merely by way of habit. This is a flaw which causes much damage; it is a kind of rust that gathers and sticks to the heart of man. That is why things that are done habitually do not have as much effect on one's life as those done after due deliberation.

Islam has so many noble characteristics that it is hard to imagine why anyone should decline to accept Islam after its excellences have been expounded and elucidated. I have given much thought to why people do not acknowledge the truth of Islam while it is so obviously possessed of such wonderful qualities. I have come to the conclusion that there is no other reason for it except one—since their early days, the non-Muslims have been hearing things about

Islam which were utterly opposed to its true principles and are full of antagonism. This is why when they are faced with the true teachings of Islam, they simply reject them. Otherwise, what other reason can there be for a Christian possessing a master's degree to fail to understand and grasp the excellences of Islam; while a person who is born in a Muslim family, no matter how uninformed and ignorant he is, easily declares Islam to be the only religion which is true and holds all others to be false. He only believes thus because his parents were Muslims, from whom at an early age he has been hearing that Islam is the only true religion. On the other hand, the one with a master's degree cannot understand it because since childhood his ears have been hearing the opposite view and therefore he is under the influence of what he has been hearing. He cannot now pay any attention to anything contrary to what he has already come to believe.

Once I had a discussion with a Christian who claimed to have done a great deal of research on atonement. He wanted to talk to me only about atonement. Complying with his request, I talked only about his desired subject. Within a few minutes, he agreed that the concept of atonement runs against reason and the law of nature. He said that he believed it only because he was born in a Christian family. In brief, many a religious ritual is performed merely out of habit. Muslims belonging to the Hanafi dispensation raise their hands after meals to offer some prayers. It is indeed commendable to say thanks to Allah in return for His bounties, but many of them are simply unaware why they are doing so. Can such people ever attain the reward which is given to those who do it purely with the intent of saying thanks to the Almighty? Never! The reward is given only when one sings the praises of His Lord from the depth of his heart. Some people complain that they offer prayers, observe fasting, give Zakat, and perform Hajj; yet they fail to attain any benefit. My answer to such people is that they only perform these acts habitually as a ritual. Why should God bestow upon them the reward that is only bestowed on true believers?

Therefore, after having heard all this, you must not think that this is only a small *laddū* which has been put before you, because the same action yields different results depending on the intent and purpose behind it. Should you understand the importance that man's intention holds, and realize how the same action on your part is rewarded differently depending upon the intent behind it, you will attain to success. There were people in Madinah who went there having migrated along with the Holy Prophet[sa], but there were also those who went there with the sole intention of doing some business. Did the later deserve any reward? Never! The reward was due only for those only who had travelled there solely for their Lord. Visiting Madinah, by itself, amounts to nothing. The reward depends upon the intent of the visit. Prayer, too, brings reward because it is offered to obey Allah and win His pleasure. Fasting too is observed because God has thus commanded it. The same is the case with Zakat and Hajj. People who have started doing all these things by way of habit only can never attain true benefit from them.

Some keep moving their hands and shoulders by way of habit. There are others, who are in the habit of saying اَلْحَمْدُ لِلّٰهِ اَلْحَمْدُ لِلّٰهِ [All praise belongs to Allah...] and سبحان اللّٰه سبحان اللّٰه [Holy is Allah...], but they do not really know why they keep uttering those words. On the other hand, should someone utter the same phrase اَلْحَمْدُ لِلّٰهِ with due intention and regard, he may become an angel in just a day.

Similarly, the phrase سبحان الله if said with the right intent and regard, can make one attain the nearness of God in a day's time. The Holy Prophet[sa] stated:

كلمتان خفيفتان على اللسان

which means: there are two sentences, which feel light on the tongue and one can utter them in a matter of seconds, but

ثقيلتان فى الميزان

that is, when weighed by God, they will be very heavy in that they will increase the weight of man's deeds, thereby bringing the scale down in his favour.

حبيبتان الى الرحمٰن

that is, these two sentences are very dear to Allah, the hearing of which pleases Him a lot. The sentences are: .

سبحان اللّٰه و بحمده سبحان اللّٰه العظيم

> Holy is Allah, with His praise. Holy is Allah, with His Greatness

There are so many people who keep saying these sentences in parrot-like fashion, but the scale of their actions remains unmoved. The Holy Prophet[sa] says that reciting them once bends the scale down on their behalf; but, in their case, even if they were to recite them a thousand times, the scale would not bend at all. Why? Because they place no intent behind their words. From their tongues, they utter that 'God is Holy', but in their hearts they pay no real attention to what they are doing. They do not thank Him in return for His bounties; rather, all they do is mere lip service to Him. As you can see, to only do things out of habit can, at times, cause great harm, and result in unimaginable consequences however good those habits may be. Let alone a good habit, even the harm of an ill habit is negated when somebody becomes accustomed to it. Those who make it a habit of eating it can eat even a full gram of arsenic, but someone who is not used to eating it can die just by consuming a grain or two. Therefore, when things become habitual, one loses the ability to distinguish between good and bad. In the Holy Quran, Allah the Almighty states:[17]

...كُلَّمَا نَضِجَتْ جُلُوْدُهُمْ بَدَّلْنٰهُمْ جُلُوْدًا غَيْرَهَا لِيَذُوْقُوا الْعَذَابَ...

> That is, when the skins of the dwellers of hell are burnt, God will give them other skins so that they may taste the punishment.

By saying so, God explains that once accustomed to something, one becomes numb to it, and so it does not remain as beneficial as it previously had been. A headache is a very painful thing, yet one who is accustomed to it, doesn't feel it as much.

---

[17] *Sūrah an-Nisā'*, 4:57

A Parable

There is a parable that explains the lack of sensitivity that results out of being used to something. It goes like this: God once said to people, 'You always complain of your difficulties to be more severe than others. You are now allowed to replace the one you think are severe with that which you consider to be less painful.' They all threw away their problems and opted for others in exchange. One person who suffered headaches, got rid of his headache and took the diseased swollen foot of someone in return. A deaf person, having thrown away his deaf ears, preferred to be blind. Similarly, everyone exchanged his pain for what he thought was not as painful. When they walked back home, the one who had opted for a heavy diseased foot felt that it was hard to take a step forward with it; the one who had opted for blindness sorrowfully missed his ears for though he could not hear but at least he could walk, but now he was simply unable to see anything. Eventually, they concluded that their previous ailments were less severe and prayed to revert to them. The point of the parable is that being accustomed to some pain makes it less painful. That is why God has stated that when the skins of the inmates of the hell will be burnt up, He will give them new ones in exchange so that their sense of suffering remains intact and they keep feeling the punishment. Those doing some good by habit do not get its true reward, and when one has become accustomed to the chastisement he is undergoing, his suffering decreases to a great degree. In other words, habits are like a bandage that covers up a wound, even though from the inside it is filled with puss.

Remember that prayers offered by way of habit are not true prayers, neither is the Zakat that is given by habit the true Zakat, nor is the fasting done by habit the true fasting and nor is the Hajj performed in this way the true Hajj. Did people not offer their prayers before the advent of the Promised Messiah[as]? Did they not give Zakat or observe fasting or perform Hajj? They did everything. But they did not do them with the true intent of doing a good deed. All their actions were just pretence. That is why they never benefited from them. As for you, whatever you do, you have only one thing to keep in view, and that is God. Should you act upon this advice, you will observe a remarkable change in your spiritual life. Therefore, abstain from doing things by way of habit. Do them with the true intent with which they should be done.

Objective of Islam

Islam's greatest object is to free you of mere ritual, which it disapproves in the strongest terms, for mere ritual in no way guarantees that one will continue doing a good deed. What Islam wants to emphasize is that whatever one does, it should be done solely for the seeking of the pleasure of God. It is then that a person gets his heart's desire. God states:[18]

كُلًّا نُّمِدُّ هٰٓؤُلَآءِ وَهٰٓؤُلَآءِ مِنْ عَطَآءِ رَبِّكَ ؕ وَمَا كَانَ عَطَآءُ
رَبِّكَ مَحْظُوْرًا ﴿۲۱﴾

---

[18] *Sūrah Banī Isrā'īl*, 17:21

That is, We extend our help to everyone. One who strives for the world, gets it; and one who strives for God, get Him. This is a blessing which is bestowed only by God, for your Lord has not shut the door of His forgiveness to anyone. Therefore, if you will strive for God, you will surely meet Him.

Stages of Spiritual Development

God has set seven stages of development for human soul. Any lack that occurs and impinges on this development occurs due to man's own habits. God, in the Holy Quran, states about the prayer:[19]

... لَاتَقْرَبُوا الصَّلٰوةَ وَاَنْتُمْ سُكٰرٰى حَتّٰى تَعْلَمُوْا مَا تَقُوْلُوْنَ ...

That is: Go not near to the prayer when you are intoxicated...

Intoxication does not simply imply drinking, since it was forbidden at that time and still is. So, when it is already forbidden, what does this injunction imply when it says that 'one should not come to the mosque being intoxicated'? There is no doubt that a drinker has also been told to not to come to the mosque, but this injunction is like that of a father who tells his ill-bred child to stay out of the home unless he mends his habits; so similar is the command in which He has prohibited a drinker from coming to the mosque. This verse has another meaning also, which is that just as a drinker is not aware of what he is saying and how he is offering his prayer,

[19] *Sūrah an-Nisā'*, 4:44

God has enjoined us not to offer our prayers merely by way of habit or because we have become accustomed to them. Your prayers should not be a result of imitating others; instead you should offer them with full consciousness and mindful of what you are doing. To do an act by way of habit or imitation—being unmindful of its true purpose—is '*sakr*'. The word '*sakr*' basically means intoxication caused by drinking wine. But the Word of God has more than one underlying meanings. Therefore, on the one hand, a drinker in this verse has been told not to go near the prayer; while on the other, it points out that one should not offer prayers being oblivious to its true purpose and objective. Just as when a drinker falls down to the ground and is not aware of his situation—for he cannot tell whether he is lying in a filthy drainage or on a well-decorated floor—likewise, he who offers the prayer merely by way of habit does not fully realize whether he is standing in the glorious court of God or in a jungle. That is why God has prohibited the offering of prayers in this way.

Seven Ranks of Spiritual Development

I will now state the seven stages of spiritual development that the Holy Quran has stated. Elaborating on these seven stages, the Holy Quran explains how if man ignores them, he falls into the abyss of spiritual deterioration; and how if he should follow them, he commences on an upward journey of continuous spiritual progress. The more understanding he gains of these stages, the more fruitful his efforts and deeds become.

First Rank

At the first stage of spirituality, man is like an inanimate substance. This is the lowest of the stages. Such people are devoid of any sense for distinguishing between right and wrong. However one tries to make them understand, all such efforts prove useless, for such people are inherently unable to progress. They do not even see dreams or receive revelation. The following verse is indicative of such people:[20]

ثُمَّ قَسَتْ قُلُوبُكُم مِّنْ بَعْدِ ذٰلِكَ فَهِيَ كَالْحِجَارَةِ اَوْ اَشَدُّ قَسْوَةً ۚ وَاِنَّ مِنَ
الْحِجَارَةِ لَمَا يَتَفَجَّرُ مِنْهُ الْاَنْهٰرُ ۚ وَاِنَّ مِنْهَا لَمَا يَشَّقَّقُ فَيَخْرُجُ مِنْهُ الْمَآءُ ۚ وَاِنَّ
مِنْهَا لَمَا يَهْبِطُ مِنْ خَشْيَةِ اللّٰهِ ۗ وَمَا اللّٰهُ بِغَافِلٍ عَمَّا تَعْمَلُوْنَ ﴿٧٥﴾

That is, these people are so corrupt that they have become like stones, and are now devoid of every seed of prosperity. Even a small seed when planted in the ground and watered, turns into a big tree; but a stone however one tries, can bring him no benefit.

Therefore, the lowest of the spiritual stages of man is the one where man is devoid of consequences for his actions and loses all sense of accountability. Islam wants to inculcate such sense and knowledge in man so that he may become conscious of what he is doing at all times, but those people who belong to this stage are not

---

[20] Then your hearts became hardened after that, till they were like stones or harder still; for of stones indeed there are some out of which gush forth streams, and of them there are some out of which flows water when they cleave asunder. And indeed, of them there are some that humble themselves for fear of Allah. And Allah is not unmindful of what you do. (*Sūrah al-Baqarah*, 2:75)

possessed of any such sense or knowledge. They are slaves to their whims and keep changing courses as it suits them. When hungry, they fill their stomachs. When they feel sleepy, they go to sleep. When they feel like having sex, they have sex. This is why they are not deserving of any reward from Allah.

Second Rank

The next stage resembles plants. Man is composed of different elements. Some elements come from non-organic matters, whereas some come from plant life and then some others from animals. That is why the most balanced diets contain elements of all three of these things. Since the body is composed of organs that develop from these elements, they exercise a kind of influence in their lives. Sometimes animalistic behaviour prevails over spiritual behaviour and man becomes like animals; whereas, at times, animalistic tendencies are suppressed and buried under the vegetable organism, and he sinks further into materialistic pursuits. Sometimes he is swayed by an influence that likens death and he takes on a character that exhibits no signs of life. His heart becomes hardened. Like a stone which can be thrown by people in any direction, he too is tossed in one direction or the other by the vicissitudes of life. Such a person becomes totally unaware of himself.

Then when one takes a step toward progress and shuns the condition that likens the dead, a kind of energy develops in him that causes him to flourish. So there are two kinds of people: those who are like stones and are devoid of any sense of life; and then there are those who are like plants and behave like sentient beings. It is now a proven fact after much experimentation that plants too have life. They certainly possess it, though it is not of such fine quality that is found in animals. To prove this, one can give the example of sensitive plant that is called *lajwantī* in Urdu, whose leaves shrink when touched. This shrub belongs to a family of plants that have reached a stage of life very close to animals. This shows that trees too are sentient, and some of them are more developed in terms of sensory perceptions than others. Similarly, some other plants also resemble animals, such as sponge whose food also is made of organic materials. Some even term the sponge as being an animal, for though it is a plant, it has developed itself to a stage that is very close to being an animal. In short, these precepts make it clear that plants too are sentient. The difference between the two is that though plants have sensory perception, they cannot protect themselves against any danger. The leaves of *lajwantī* or touch-me-not do shrink when they are touched, but are not capable of running away from danger to save them. Likewise, a person sometimes may not be fully devoid of spirituality, yet he is unable to safeguard himself against any attack of sinfulness. This is due to his being depleted of spirituality. The Holy Quran speaks of such people in the following verse:[21]

وَإِنْ تَدْعُوهُمْ إِلَى الْهُدَىٰ لَا يَسْمَعُوا ۖ وَتَرَاهُمْ يَنْظُرُونَ إِلَيْكَ وَهُمْ لَا يُبْصِرُونَ ﴿١٩٩﴾

[21] *Sūrah al-A'rāf*, 7:199

> Meaning that these opponents are such that you invite them to guidance, but they hear not. You think they have the ability to see, but the fact is that they see nothing.

The literal meaning is to hear, but the purpose of hearing is to obey. That is why لَا يَسْمَعُوا implies that they will not believe, and that they simply do not have the ability to acquire faith. Indeed these are people who, though possessed of some spirituality, are unable to protect themselves. Having eyes, they are unable to benefit from them.

Third Rank

Then there is a stage higher than this, which is the animal stage. At this stage, man tends to behave like animals, in that he is a more conscious being than plants are. Should someone call him, he is able to hear, but will not be able to understand. Should you decide to injure him, he will run away, but still cannot fully provide for himself means that can permanently protect him against such harm. It is natural on the part of man to keep thinking of ways to get rid of those things which he considers harmful; but as for animals, they are simply unable to create anything or make any progress. Regarding such people, God says:[22]

... لَهُمْ قُلُوبٌ لَّا يَفْقَهُونَ بِهَا وَلَهُمْ أَعْيُنٌ لَّا يُبْصِرُونَ بِهَا وَلَهُمْ
آذَانٌ لَّا يَسْمَعُونَ بِهَا ۚ أُولَٰئِكَ كَالْأَنْعَامِ بَلْ هُمْ أَضَلُّ ۚ أُولَٰئِكَ هُمُ الْغَافِلُونَ ﴿١٨٠﴾

---

[22] *Sūrah al-Aʿrāf*, 7:180

That is: they have hearts, but they do not benefit themselves therewith. They have eyes, but they avail themselves not therewith. They have ears, but they do not use them to their advantage. They have all these things, but lack human wisdom. Instead, they only possess such wisdom as is found in animals. When faced with fear, they take to their heels, but are unable to find means to protect themselves in future.

This means they prostrate at the Divine threshold when faced with fear and trepidation and manage to protect themselves against such suffering, but are unable to protect themselves permanently. They turn to God only when they are hit with some calamity.

Fourth Rank

After this stage, one enters another stage where he becomes more conscientious. This is a stage that lies at the midpoint. There are three more stages after it, and three before it. At this stage, man becomes a conscious being and is fully aware and cognizant of his actions, though at times he is completely overtaken by Satan. This means that sometimes he is drawn towards vice and sometimes towards good; but he is not easily overpowered by vice, for he has developed the ability to recognize evil. About this state of man, God says:[23]

إِنَّ الَّذِيْنَ اتَّقَوْا إِذَا مَسَّهُمْ طٰٓئِفٌ مِّنَ الشَّيْطٰنِ تَذَكَّرُوْا فَإِذَا هُمْ مُّبْصِرُوْنَ ﴿٢٠٢﴾

[23] *Sūrah al-A'rāf*, 7:202

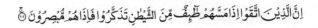

> *As to* those who are righteous, when a suggestion from Satan assails them, they remember *God*: and behold! they begin to see *things rightly*.

This is the stage of man where he is prone to forgetfulness. In other words, we can call this stage as *nafs-e-lawwāmah*, or the reproving self. About such people God says that they quickly seek refuge with Allah if they are ever attacked by Satan, and this is what the righteous should always do.

Fifth Rank

Thereafter, man progresses further and advances to the point where he becomes like an angel. He becomes so watchful that Satan is no longer able to overpower him. His knowledge about God increases to a degree that he begins to act upon all of His commandments, and just as angels work in accordance with يَفْعَلُوْنَ مَا يُؤْمَرُوْنَ, he too fulfils his obligations in terms of every Divine commandment. At this stage, forgetfulness can never overtake him. Indicating this, God says:[24]

[24] *Sūrah ar-Ra'd*, 13:20–25

اَفَمَنْ يَّعْلَمُ اَنَّمَآ اُنْزِلَ اِلَيْكَ مِنْ رَّبِّكَ الْحَقُّ كَمَنْ هُوَ اَعْمٰى ۭ اِنَّمَا يَتَذَكَّرُ
اُولُوا الْاَلْبَابِ ۙ﴿٢٠﴾ الَّذِيْنَ يُوْفُوْنَ بِعَهْدِ اللّٰهِ وَلَا يَنْقُضُوْنَ الْمِيْثَاقَ ۙ﴿٢١﴾ وَالَّذِيْنَ
يَصِلُوْنَ مَآ اَمَرَ اللّٰهُ بِهٖٓ اَنْ يُّوْصَلَ وَ يَخْشَوْنَ رَبَّهُمْ وَيَخَافُوْنَ سُوْٓءَ
الْحِسَابِ ۭ﴿٢٢﴾ وَالَّذِيْنَ صَبَرُوا ابْتِغَآءَ وَجْهِ رَبِّهِمْ وَاَقَامُوا الصَّلٰوةَ وَاَنْفَقُوْا مِمَّا
رَزَقْنٰهُمْ سِرًّا وَّعَلَانِيَةً وَّيَدْرَءُوْنَ بِالْحَسَنَةِ السَّيِّئَةَ اُولٰٓئِكَ لَهُمْ عُقْبَى
الدَّارِ ۙ﴿٢٣﴾ جَنّٰتُ عَدْنٍ يَّدْخُلُوْنَهَا وَمَنْ صَلَحَ مِنْ اٰبَآئِهِمْ وَاَزْوَاجِهِمْ
وَذُرِّيّٰتِهِمْ وَالْمَلٰٓئِكَةُ يَدْخُلُوْنَ عَلَيْهِمْ مِّنْ كُلِّ بَابٍ ﴿٢٤﴾ سَلٰمٌ عَلَيْكُمْ بِمَا
صَبَرْتُمْ فَنِعْمَ عُقْبَى الدَّارِ ۭ﴿٢٥﴾

That is, O Prophet, who knows that what has been revealed to you from your Lord is the truth, how can you be like that blind person who does not consider it to be true? Only those truly benefit from Our words who are gifted with understanding—that is, those who are filled with wisdom and insight. They fulfil their covenants with Allah and do not break them. They follow what God commands them to do and fear their Lord. They dread the evil reckoning. They persevere in seeking the pleasure of their Lord, observe prayer and spend out of what they have been given, secretly and openly. They exert to repel evil with good, and spread goodness. It is these who shall have the best reward in the paradise. Their abode there will be everlasting. They are blessed with such a high spiritual station that their reward will not be confined to them. Many of their relatives who might not have been able to do enough good [in this world] will be elevated in rank due to them. Their relatives will be provided an abode where they themselves will be. This will happen because they tried to make the people righteous and made efforts to bring them to the right path. In return for what they did,

God will not only raise their own spiritual stations, but will also raise the stations of those related to them.

The Holy Prophet[sa] has said: In paradise, I will be accompanied by Ali and Fatimah. That is because God says that He will be kind to even the relatives of those who look after His creation in this world. The next statement by God is very wonderful. Everything is attracted to its own kind. God states that when these people will enter paradise, the angels will swiftly move towards them. The angels are bound to fall in love with them, for they are those possessed of angelic spirits. They will rush towards them saying, 'peace be on you, for you remained steadfast'. Here, God has stated in clear terms that such people will possess the station equal to that of the angels—and the station possessed by the angels is indeed very high.

Sixth Rank

Man, then, progresses further and excels even higher when he becomes aware of his spiritual station. It is then that he does not only safeguard his self against vice; he rather comes to understand that his being is mere nothing. Having realized this, he surrenders himself completely to God. It is this state of man about which the sufi's have said that man begins to partake of divine attributes.

The Holy Quran has thus elaborated this rank:[25]

[25] Nay, whoever submits himself completely to Allah, while he is excellent in conduct, shall have his reward with his Lord. No fear *shall come* upon such, neither shall they grieve. (*Sūrah al-Baqarah*, 2:113)

بَلٰى ۚ مَنۡ اَسۡلَمَ وَجۡهَهٗ لِلّٰهِ وَهُوَ مُحۡسِنٌ فَلَهٗۤ اَجۡرُهٗ عِنۡدَ رَبِّهٖ ۪ وَلَا خَوۡفٌ عَلَيۡهِمۡ وَلَا هُمۡ يَحۡزَنُوۡنَ ﴿۱۱۳﴾

Ḥaḍrat Ibrāhīm[as] [Abraham], who was a Prophet of God, reached this stage. Allah says about him:[26]

اِذۡ قَالَ لَهٗ رَبُّهٗۤ اَسۡلِمۡ ۙ قَالَ اَسۡلَمۡتُ لِرَبِّ الۡعٰلَمِيۡنَ ﴿۱۳۲﴾

That is, when God said: اَسۡلِمۡ [submit], Ḥaḍrat Ibrāhīm[as] replied with اَسۡلَمۡتُ لِرَبِّ الۡعٰلَمِيۡنَ [I have submitted to the Lord of the worlds]. Hence, one station of man was such that he can be counted as being from among the angels. At that stage he thought he could do something so he asked for an order to be given. But this is a station at which one says that he is mere nothing, and that he will act as commanded by God. Now, since he will act as God tells him to act, all of his actions will be God's actions; for the pen only inscribes what the writer wills.

It is said that there was a soldier who would move his sword so quickly and forcefully that he could cut all four legs of a horse with one stroke. When the king's son saw the scene, he asked for the sword. The man was hesitant to give it to him, but the king asked him to hand over the sword to the boy. When the prince moved the sword, nothing happened. The soldier said that the reason he did not want to give him the sword was that there was nothing so special about the sword. He said that the sword would cut all four legs of the horse because of the hands that were using it. Even if he

---

26 *Sūrah al-Baqarah*, 2:132

were given another sword, he could still demonstrate the same, for there was nothing special about the sword; rather, it was his own hand wielding it that possessed the strength to cut. The same is the condition of man when he hands himself over to God. All his actions then become God's actions. This is the reason that some foolish people, who fail to understand this phenomenon and try to impede the work of such people, are absolutely annihilated. One, who has attained this station, is no longer in need of any angels.

It is related about Ḥaḍrat Ibrāhīm[as] that the angel Gabriel visited him and asked if he needed anything. He replied if he needed anything, he would ask directly from God. At this the angel Gabriel told him to pray. Abraham replied, 'Isn't God aware of my circumstances? Why should I pray? When God is already aware of all my needs, why should I ask Him for anything?' In short, while on the path of spiritual progress, man goes so far that he ascends above and beyond even the angelic qualities. He then becomes an embodiment of divine attributes, and gives himself into the hands of God like a weapon which moves and strikes as God will. To challenge such a person is to invite a contest with God. Every action of such a person is devoted to seeking Allah's pleasure. It is this spiritual station of which the Holy Prophet[sa] said that when man, having progressed, comes to be so close to God, God becomes his ears, hands and feet. The one, who becomes his enemy, becomes an enemy to God; and one who becomes friends with him, becomes friends with God. It was to this station in view of which God said to the Promised Messiah[as]: 'one who pays not heed to you, in fact he is heedless of me, for My attributes have manifested in you. For this reason, to denounce you is equal to denouncing me.' This is a station at which man is completely overtaken by his Lord.

Seventh Rank

There is only one station higher than this, and it is described by God as:[27]

...ثُمَّ اَنْشَاْنٰهُ خَلْقًا اٰخَرَ...

It is very hard to describe this spiritual state. At this station, man is granted a new creation, and is once again blessed with new faculties. At the stage earlier than this, he spoke when God told him to speak; but at this stage he is blessed with such an elevated station and purity of heart that Allah the Almighty turns whatever he utters into a Divine decree. At this stage, man becomes a beloved of God. That is why many words which such people speak out of their own inference are fulfilled by God. This is what has been indicated in this verse:[28]

قُلْ اِنْ كُنْتُمْ تُحِبُّوْنَ اللّٰهَ فَاتَّبِعُوْنِيْ يُحْبِبْكُمُ اللّٰهُ وَيَغْفِرْ لَكُمْ ذُنُوْبَكُمْ ؕ وَاللّٰهُ غَفُوْرٌ رَّحِيْمٌ ۝٣٢

That is, O Prophet! Say to them 'I am the beloved of God, and if you also wish to be loved by Him, then follow me.'

---

27 ...then We developed it into another creation. (*Sūrah al-Mu'minūm*, 23:15)

28 Say, 'If you love Allah, follow me: then will Allah love you and forgive you your faults. And Allah is Most Forgiving, Merciful.' (*Sūrah Al-e-'Imran*, 3:165)

At this stage, man is not only an embodiment of Divine attributes, his spiritual progress attains to a point where he severs his ties with all other things beside God, and one cannot reach God except through him.

In short, these are the stages of man's spiritual senses which God has illustrated in the Holy Quran. The more one excels in them, the more his spiritual station is raised. The Holy Prophet[sa] had attained to such a high stage of spiritual progress that he described it as:

تنام عينى ولاينام قلبى

or that 'my eyes asleep, but my heart is always awake.' He would sleep sometimes, but then offer the prayers without making ablution. His heart was blessed with such transcendent spiritual enlightenment that his senses would remain absolutely pure even while asleep. That is why when he was asked why he had started the prayer without making ablution, whereas before that he was snoring during the sleep. He said, 'My eyes sleep, but the heart remains awake.' He would always be in such a state of vision that many a time he would get to know the inner state of the hearts of those offering prayers behind him. This is evident from the authentic *aḥādīth*. Hence, when in such a state of spiritual enlightenment, one can never suffer remissness. God has thus spoken of this stage:[29]

وَمَا يَنْطِقُ عَنِ الْهَوٰى ۞ اِنْ هُوَ اِلَّا وَحْيٌ يُّوْحٰى ۞

[29] *Sūrah an-Najam*, 53:4–5

> That is, When someone becomes Our true servant, then his words are not his but Ours. He no longer speaks from his own desire.

This stage marks the pinnacle of human excellence. I advise you that if you desire spiritual progress, you should try to enhance your spiritual senses. Sin takes birth when one is devoid of these spiritual senses. Take for instance prostitutes. They too give alms, but do they get the reward? No, never! The reason is that their alms are not based on a desire to seek divine pleasure; rather it is to avert punishment. If their alms were based on the true intent for seeking divine pleasure and fear of the Almighty, why would they commit adultery in the first place?

About Ḥaḍrat Abu Bakr[ra] the Holy Prophet[sa] said, 'He has not gained excellence due to prayers; rather on account of that which lies in his heart.' As for prayers, they were offered by other people as well. Even today, we see non-Aḥmadīs offering prayers. Let alone the stage attained by the Companions of the Prophet[sa], do they attain to the stage of even an ordinary believer? They are not even worthy of the rewards that can be attained by performing minor services to the believer. In fact, most of them are wicked and sinful. There is no other reason for their being unrighteous except that they are not conscious of what they are doing.

You need to be conscious of what you do. None of your actions should be based on mere habit or tradition. Instead, all of them should be performed with a view to seeking divine pleasure. For your convenience, I must also elaborate here the ways to achieve this goal; but before I speak of them, I must also explain that some people suffer a serious misunderstanding.

A Misunderstanding

As soon as some people take the oath of allegiance they start asking why they are unable to see God. Should someone ask them how many years it takes one to acquire a Masters' degree, their answer would be 'not less than sixteen years'. I now ask such people while they have to spend sixteen full years to acquire worldly knowledge, why do they begin asking such questions after they have spent merely a day in learning about God? One can never become an M.A. on the first day of his education at school—no matter how much he wants to be so. Such people, having offered the prayers only for a few days, start asking why God does not come to their help. Why do their enemies not suffer defeat and humiliation? Surprising indeed is their haste! How soon do they wish to attain spiritual excellence! Months are spent in waiting for the crops to be ready, and sixteen long years are spent working hard and striving to attain the degree of M.A. Even a baby takes nine months after conception to be born.

Is there anything that can be achieved without working hard, exerting effort and sparing time for it? With every noteworthy blessing there is attached some hardship and difficulty. You must, therefore, remember that as one has to strive hard and work continuously to attain worldly gains, so has he to do in case of his religious obligations. The harder one works, the better gains one achieves. Someone may ask what difference is there between Islam and other religions if success is wholly dependent upon one's own effort and hard work. My answer to him would be that one who wants to go to Batala, and takes the road that leads to Batala, will ultimately reach Batala even if he gets tired after a few miles; but the one who will leave in the opposite direction will never be able to reach Batala even if he continues to walk all his life. You, too, will only get to your desired destination if you tread upon the path that I have laid down for you. Otherwise, you will never get there. You can never reach God unless you have the true intention to reach Him, and the one who intends to find Him, will ultimately find Him. God says in the Holy Quran:[30]

وَالَّذِيْنَ جَاهَدُوْا فِيْنَا لَنَهْدِيَنَّهُمْ سُبُلَنَا...

> That is, those who are always busy striving in Our path and doing jihad against their selves and fighting against vice to reach us, We will surely guide such h people to the path that lead to Us.

There is a point of deep wisdom here that needs to be remembered. Allah the Almighty says here: سُبُلَنَا, or Our ways; but at another point He said وَاَنَّ هٰذَا صِرَاطِيْ مُسْتَقِيْمًا, which means that 'this is the only way which leads straight to Me.' This is indicative of the fact that there also exist ways that are misleading. But the word سُبُلَنَا indicates that there are a number of ways leading to God. These verses would mean when read together that after following one way, there can be two or three or even more paths; yet, they do not run contrary to each other. However, since one way is to be followed by another, one will have to make their utmost efforts to traverse all of them. Only then will one be able to reach the destination.

---

[30] *Sūrah al-'Ankabūt*, 29:70

It is this jihad which you need to perform. I now explain the ways that have been set out by the Holy Quran in this regard.

1. First is prayer, which, if offered five times a day by someone with even an iota of sincerity, will transform him altogether with the grace of Allah.
2. Second is Zakat. One, who, under Divine commandment, draws out a portion from his wealth once a year, remains conscious of the fact that he can sacrifice his wealth for God.
3. Third is fasting, which teaches one to give preference to religion even if in doing that he has to suffer and undergo hardship.
4. Fourth is Hajj, which creates in man a sense of sacrifice that in case he ever has to permanently depart from his dear ones, relatives, country, wealth and property, for the pleasure of God, he is able to do that.

Another remedy which God has prescribed for this is the Holy Quran which brings man out of every darkness. Darkness is marked with carelessness and lassitude. That is why sleep is not so overwhelming during the day time. Due to the study of the Holy Quran one experiences a sense of wakefulness and alertness, but one has to reflect deeply and delve into its meanings so that one is not misled while translating it. When translating the Holy Quran, you must remember the following:

1. Do not accept an interpretation of a verse that contradicts other verses. Verses which can have multiple interpretations

should be interpreted in the light of those having no ambiguity.

2. Do not take a verse to mean something contrary to the meanings as explained to us by the Holy Prophet[sa].
3. Do not take a verse to mean something contrary to the Arabic lexicon.
4. Do not take a verse to mean what is not supported by the grammatical rules of the Arabic language. There are people who ask why God should take grammatical rules into account. They argue that God is not bound by any grammar. They fail to realize that though God is not bound, we poor fellows are. Should the Word of God be incomprehensible to us, what benefit can we acquire from it? It was indeed due to this lack of knowledge about grammar that Maulavī Muhammad Ali, the leader of the disbelievers of *Khilāfat* translated قُلِ اللّٰهُ ۙ ثُمَّ ذَرْهُمْ as 'make the people believe in God and then let them go'. The word 'Allah' was punctuated with a vowel point *paish* but he took it to be *zabar,* thus translating it wrongly.
5. Do not interpret a verse to have meanings that are contrary to those illustrated by the Promised Messiah[as] whom God has sent as *Ḥakam* [Adjudicator]and *'Adl* [Arbitrator].
6. Do not accept meanings which are not sanctioned by another verse or are against wisdom and rationality, but if the meanings are clearly supported by the actual events as they unfolded, then do not let rationality interfere with them. However, the exposition in such cases should be based on by wisdom and rationality.

7. Do not interpret a verse to have meanings which portray the Word of God and His Action to be contrary to each other. I wished to give a detailed speech on how we can interpret the Holy Quran correctly, but due to shortage of time and a throat illness I am not able to do so. Should God enable me to do so, I shall speak on this subject at some other time.

Then God commanded:[31]

يٰٓاَيُّهَا الَّذِيْنَ اٰمَنُوا اذْكُرُوا اللّٰهَ ذِكْرًا كَثِيْرًا ۙ﴿٤٢﴾ وَّسَبِّحُوْهُ بُكْرَةً وَّاَصِيْلًا ﴿٤٣﴾
هُوَ الَّذِيْ يُصَلِّيْ عَلَيْكُمْ وَمَلٰٓئِكَتُهٗ لِيُخْرِجَكُمْ مِّنَ الظُّلُمٰتِ اِلَى النُّوْرِ ؕ وَكَانَ
بِالْمُؤْمِنِيْنَ رَحِيْمًا ﴿٤٤﴾

That is, O ye who believe! Remember Allah with much remembrance. And glorify Him in the morning and evening. He it is who sends blessings on you, and so do His angels, so that He may bring you out of darkness into light. And He is Merciful to the believers.

The Holy Prophet[sa], in light of this verse, has told the believers to recite a number of prayers.

سبحان اللّٰہ و بحمده سبحان اللّٰہ العظيم ـ اللهم اسلمت نفسى اليك ووجهت و جهى
اليك ـــ رغبةً ورهبةً اليك لا ملجاو لا منجى منك الا اليك امنت بكتا بك الذى انزلت
و نبيك الذى ارسلت

[31] *Sūrah al-Aḥzḥb*, 33:42–45

The Holy Prophet[sa] enjoined every believer to recite these prayers every night before going to bed, and not to talk thereafter. If you want progress, you must recite them. I now come to its meanings. By saying so, man declares:

> 'O my Lord! I entrust to You everything that belongs to me. I entrust my life to You. Now as I am going to sleep, I do not know if I will get up in the morning. Therefore, I entrust all my affairs to You, for I know it is You who will give me the reward, and should I do against my declaration, I will be punished. I have no other place to seek refuge and protect myself against Your punishment. Indeed I have no other choice but to fall in prostration at your threshold again even if I am punished by you. O my Lord! Be my witness that I believe in the Book you have revealed and the Prophet that you have sent. (*Bukhārī, Kitābud-Da'wāt*)

In short, the Holy Prophet Muhammad, may peace and blessings of Allah be upon him, has enjoined the believers to recite a number of prayers, but our Jamā'at is not paying enough attention to them. I advise you to attend to this matter, but you must do so with a solemn intention. Perform all actions only in view of seeking divine pleasure. May Allah render all the members of our Jamā'at to become pious and God-fearing. May heedlessness disappear from the world, and may the people be able to see the countenance of that Dear Lord, having beheld whom one can simply not turn towards anybody else. *Āmīn*.

GLOSSARY

Ahmadiyya Muslim Jamā'at—The Community of Muslims who have accepted the claims of Ḥaḍrat Mirza Ghulam Ahmad[as] of Qadian as the Promised Messiah and Mahdi. The Community was established by Ḥaḍrat Mirza Ghulam Ahmad[as] in 1889, and is now under the leadership of his fifth *Khalīfah*—Ḥaḍrat Mirza Masroor Ahmad (may Allah be his help). The Community is also known as **Jamā'at-e-Ahmadiyya**. A member of the Community is called an **Ahmadi Muslim** or simply an **Ahmadī**.

Alḥamdulillāh—A phrase from the Holy Quran meaning, all praise belongs to Allah alone.

Allah—Allah is the personal name of God in Islam. To show proper reverence to Him, Muslims often add *Ta'ālā*, translated here as 'the Exalted', when saying His Holy name.

Anjuman—An administrative body established by the Promised Messiah[as] for the administration of the affairs of the Ahmadiyya Muslim Community.

Bai'at—Oath of allegiance to a religious leader; initiation at the hands of a Prophet or his *Khalīfah*.

Bukhārī—A book of *āḥādith* (the sayings) of the Holy Prophet Muhammad[sa] compiled by Ḥaḍrat Imam Muhammad Bin Isma'il Bukhari[rh] (194H-256H). This book of *āḥādith* is believed to be the most authentic book after the Holy Quran.

Darsul-Quran—Meetings or classes for the study of the Holy Quran.

Ḥaḍrat—A term of respect used for a person of established righteousness and piety.

Muṣleḥ-e-Mau'ūd—A title used by Ahmadi Muslims to refer to Ḥaḍrat Mirza Bashirud Din Mahmud Ahmad, Khalīfatul-Masīḥ II[ra].

Hadith—A saying of the Holy Prophet Muhammad[sa]. The plural is *āḥādith*.

Holy Prophet[sa]—A term used exclusively for the Founder of Islam, Ḥaḍrat Muhammad, may peace and blessings of Allah be upon him.

Holy Quran—The Book sent by Allah for the guidance of mankind. It was revealed word by word to the Holy Prophet Muhammad[sa] over a period of twenty-three years.

Imam Mahdī—The title given to the Promised Reformer by the Holy Prophet Muhammad[sa]; it means: the Guided Leader.

Istikhārah—A special Prayer made to seek guidance from Allah before making an important decision.

Jalsah Salānāh—Annual convention or gathering of the Ahmadiyya Muslim Community. It was initiated by the Promised Massiah[as] himself.

Jamā'at—Jamā'at means community. Although the word *jamā'at* itself may refer to any community, in this book, Jamā'at specifically refers to the Ahmadiyya Muslim Jamā'at.

Khalīfah and Khilāfat—Caliph is derived from the Arabic word *Khalīfah*, which herein means the successor. *Khulafā'* is the plural of *Khalīfah*. In Islamic terminology, the title *'Khalīfa-e-Rāshid'* [righteous *Khalīfah*] is applied to one of the first four *khulafā'* who continued the mission of the Holy Prophet Muhammad[sa]. Ahmadi Muslims refer to each successor of the Promised Messiah[as] as Khalīfatul-Masīḥ. The institution of successorship is called *Khilāfat*.

Khalīfatul-Masīḥ I—Ḥaḍrat Khalīfatul-Masīḥ I, Ḥakīm Maulānā Nurud-Din[ra] (1841–1914), the first person to do the *bai'at* at the hand of the Promised Messiah[as], was elected as the first *Khalīfah* after the demise of the Promised Messiah[as]. The Promised Messiah[as] has highly appreciated his faith, sincerity and sacrifices and has regarded him as a model for everybody in the ummah.

Khalīfatul-Masīḥ II—Ḥaḍrat Khalīfatul-Masīḥ II, Mirza Bashir-ud-Din Mahmud Ahmad[ra] (1889–1965), was the second successor of the Promised Messiah[as]. He is also called Muṣleḥ-e-Mau'ūd because he was born in accordance with the prophecy made by the Promised Messiah[as] in 1886 concerning the birth of a righteous son who would be endowed with unique abilities and attributes.

Khalīfatul-Masīḥ III—Ḥaḍrat Khalīfatul-Masīḥ III, Ḥāfiz Mirzā Nāsir Ahmad[rh] (1909–1982), was the grandson of the Promised Messiah[as] and his third successor. Before being elected as *Khalīfah*, he served in many key positions in the Jamā'at.

Khalīfatul-Masīḥ IV—Ḥaḍrat Khalīfatul-Masīḥ IV, Mirza Tahir Ahmad[rh] (1928–2003), was the fourth successor of the Promised Messiah[as]. He was the grandson of the Founder of the Ahmadiyya Muslim Jamā'at, Ḥaḍrat Mirza Ghulam Ahmad, the Promised Messiah[as].

Khalīfatul-Masīḥ V—Ḥaḍrat Khalīfatul-Masīḥ V, Mirza Masroor Ahmad[aa], is the fifth successor of the Promised Messiah[as] and the current Imam of Jamā'at-e-Ahmadiyya. He is the great grandson of the Promised Messiah[as].

Khilāfat—The institution of successorship in Islam. *See also* **Khalīfah.**

Khulafā'—Plural of **Khalīfah.** *See also* **Khalīfah.**

Mināratul-Masīḥ—A minaret in the Aqsa Mosque of Qadian, which was initiated by the Promised Messiah[as] and completed during the *Khilāfat* of Ḥaḍrat Khalīfatul-Masīḥ II[ra]

Mahdi—'The guided one.' This is the title given by the Holy Prophet Muhammad[sa] to the awaited Reformer of the Latter Days.

Maulānā or Maulavī—A Muslim religious cleric.

Nikāḥ—The announcement of marriage in Islam.

Muhammad—Proper name of the Holy Prophet[sa] of Islam.

The Promised Messiah—This term refers to the Founder of the Ahmadiyya Muslim Jamā'at, Ḥaḍrat Mirza Ghulam Ahmad[as] of Qadian. He claimed that he had been sent by Allah in accordance with the prophecies of the Holy Prophet[sa] about the coming of *al-Imam al-Mahdi* (the Guided Leader) and Messiah.

Sunnah—Traditions of the Holy Prophet Muhammad[sa] of Islam.

Sūrah—A term in Arabic referring to a chapter of the Holy Quran.

Shariah—Religious law.

INDEX

Allah
all-encompassing knowledge of, 152
beauty and grandeur of, 144
Creator of all things of beauty, 142
Eternal, Ever-lasting, and the Sustainer of all, 147
ever awake and vigilant, 148
glorification of, taught by the Holy Prophet Muhammad[sa], 162
Grandeur and Glory of, 154
Greatness and Beauty of, 154
our only object and desire, 141
two kinds of manifestation of power, 17
Anjuman
defined, 9
rebellion by, foretold in a vision, 51
role not the same as Khalīfah, 9
Āryas
impact of politics on, 81
atonement
concept against reason and law of nature, 160
Āyatul-Kursī
meanings of, 145
British Government
importance of gratitude to, 83
congregational Prayers
importance of, 116
correspondence school
need for, 126
death of Jesus[as]
proof of, 30
gambling and drinking
drawbacks of, far outnumber the benefits, 72
prohibition of, 72
God. See *Allah*
habit
prayer and Zakat by way of, not meritorious, 165
Ḥaḍrat 'Īsā[ra] (Jesus)
admonitions to Simon Peter, 15
Khilāfat after, 14

Ḥaḍrat Abū Bakr Ṣiddīq[ra]
decision to proceed with the expedition to Syria, 117
his *khilāfat* as a manifestation of divine power, 17
on Zakat, 117
Ḥaḍrat Ādam[as]
lessons from the story of, 142
Ḥaḍrat Ali[ra]
appointment of Ḥaḍrat Hasan as Khalīfah by, 27
seen in a dream of the Promised Messiah, 37
Ḥaḍrat Ibrāhīm[as]
trust in Allah of, 177
Ḥaḍrat Khalīfatul-Masīḥ II[ra]
dream about the demise of Ḥaḍrat Khalīfatul-Masīḥ I[ra], 58
had no desire to be elected, 25
never wanted to be a *Khalīfah*, 67
steps to maintain unity in the Jamā'at, 25
Ḥaḍrat Khalīfatul-Masīḥ I[ra]
emphasis upon divine will in the appointment of *Khalīfah*, 50
emphasis upon the need of *Khilāfat* by, 50
exposed the hypocrisy of people who objected to *Khilāfat*, 55
sickness of, 20
story narrated by, of the people of Bhopal, 142
Ḥaḍrat Mūsa[as] (Moses)
grief of Israelites on the death of, 18
Ḥaḍrat Usman[ra]
views about the robe of Khilāfat, 28
heavenly testimony
about *Khilāfat*, 48
Holy Prophet Muhammad[sa]
bounties of Allah on, 91
heavy burden of Prophethood, 8
on who is honoured, 107
work of, 9
Holy Quran
every Ahmadi should have a copy of, 125
need for classes to teach, 125
translation of, in other languages, 129
human intellect
not infallible, 69
idolatry
misdirected expressions of love can lead to, 4
Imam Hasan[ra]
abandonment of *Khilāfat* by, 27
Islam
challenges faced by, 78
istikhārah
defined, 70
need and importance of, 70

Jamā'at-e-Ahmadiyya
a grouping of the elect of God, 156
Jesus. *See* Ḥaḍrat 'Īsā
parable of the prodigal son, 33
Khalīfah
connotation in Arabic language, 13
defined, 7
need not be a king, 11
need not be directly appointed by God, 11
need of for maintaining unity, 22
popular misunderstandings about the term, 11
Khawaja Kamalud-Din
dramatic health improvement after passing law examination, 8
Khilāfat
burden of, 7
example of the grand consensus after the demise of the Promised Messiah, 30
functions of, 9
heavy burden of, 5, 28
means of true sympathy, love and prayers for the followers of, 6
misunderstandings about, 10
no hereditary inheritance of, 28
no infringement upon the freedom of followers, 6
personal account of, 5
personal feelings of Ḥaḍrat Muṣleḥ Mau'ūd about, 6
the central point in the controversies about, 47
two types of, 13
knowledge
constantly undergoing change, 69
Kufw
issue of, in marriage, 92
marriages
between Aḥmadīs and non-Aḥmadīs, 92
issue of tribal and family considerations, 98
reasons causing delay of, 95
sanctity and importance of, 94
Maulavī Abdur-Rahman
martyrdom prophesied by a revelation, 38
Maulavī Muhammad Ali
avoidance of serious discussion about *Khilāfat*, 25
decision to leave Qadian, 24
efforts of his friends failed, 66
incident at the Nūr Mosque, 23
seen in a dream by Ḥaḍrat Khalīfatul-Masīḥ II[ra], 65

Minaratul-Masih
important landmark of the time of the Promised Messiah[as], 128
Mir Muhammad Ishaq
questions on *Khilāfat* prepared by, given to Ḥaḍrat Khalīfatul-Masīḥ I[ra], 54
Mount Sinai
Ḥaḍrat Musa[ra] (Moses) and, 26
Muhyud-Dīn Ibni Arabi[rh]
on similarity as reason for companionship, 105
Muslim League
comments of the Promised Messiah about, 74
membership of Khwaja Kamalud Din in, 74
Nawwāb Muhammad Ali Khan
announcement of the will of Ḥaḍrat Khalīfatul-Masīḥ I[ra] by, 60
nobility
criterion of, 109
noble intentions
importance of, 158
Nūr Mosque
gathering in, for election of Khalīfah, 22
objective of Islam, 165
ordeals
cannot cause a heavenly movement to die, 36
Peter
given specific role by Jesus, 16
piety
the only consideration of honour, 103
politics
demands too much time, 78
impact of, on Āryas, 81
involves grouping and lobbying, 80
merges the smaller parties into the larger ones, 80
need to stay away from, 70
why many people are attracted to it, 77
Prayer
importance of, in congregation, 114
Prayers, of *'Ishā* and *Fajr*
special emphasis laid upon, 116
preachers
need for, 125
primary schools
need for, 124
Promised Messiah[as]
exhortations for propagation, 19
granted permission to intercede for Nawwāb Abdur-Rahim, 151
mention of Khulafā' in *al-Waṣiyyat*, 16
need to preserve the life history of, 122

never asked his followers to indulge in, 71
noted the vision of Hadrat Khalifatul Masih II in his notebook, 52
prayer for Nawwāb Abdur-Rahim, 150
prophecies about the conflict over *Khilāfat*, 37
revelation of committing everything to Allah, 31
tests for the books of, 127

Prophet
only the one appointed by God, 3

Prophethood
why granted at the age of forty, 7

reconciliation
only on the basis of truth, 35

robe of Khilāfat
dire consequences of abandoning, 27

Sayyed Abdul-Latif Shaheed
martyrdom prophesied by a revelation, 38

settlement of disputes
system of, in the Jamā'at, 124

Sheikh Rahmatullah
revelation of the Promised Messiah about, 41

Sikhs
atrocities during the rule of, in the Punjab, 84

spiritual development
seven ranks of, 167
stages of, 166

success
recipe for, in the Holy Quran, 90

terminology and etiquettes
importance of using appropriate, 3

The Holy Prophet Muhammad[sa]
on status, 106

tribes
philosophy behind the division into, 103

Tyranny
Holy Prophet Muhammad[sa]'s admonitions in the face of, 75

Zakat
benefits of, 119
importance of, 117
not due on things taxed by the government, 118
purification of money through, 122